Praise for this edition of

Family Flourishing

The True Meaning of Wealth

BY

James E. Hughes Jr.
Mary K. Duke
Stacy L. Allred

Finally, a practical guide to making wealth truly work for the family. This book helps families see how wealth can serve not only prosperity, but also purpose, values, and well-being across generations—and invites advisors to support that deeper work.

— Dennis Jaffe
Thought leader and monthly contributor
to *Forbes* on family business & wealth

The must-read book family inheritors, trustees, and advisors have been waiting for: a practical guide to the most difficult question: how to help families flourish in the context of great financial capital.

— Scott Peppet
President, Chai Trust Company

On the eve of the largest intergenerational wealth transfer in history, *Family Flourishing* arrives as a seminal work. Starting with the bold claim that the true meaning of wealth is not money, but well-being, the authors deftly integrate deep wisdom about the "why" with practical and heartfelt guidance on the "how." This is a work of love of the highest order.

— Matthew T. Lee, PhD
Director of the Flourishing Network and
Human Flourishing Program, Harvard University

Few people have shaped the conversation about family wealth more profoundly than Jay Hughes, and in *Family Flourishing,* Jay and his co-authors have written the book our field has needed: a rigorous, yet compassionate framework for what it actually means for a family to flourish.

It is practical, deeply human, and long overdue – a book that challenges families and their advisors to ask the harder questions that legal documents alone can never answer. This is essential reading for family members, trustees, and advisors focused not just on the family's financial prosperity but on its long-term continuity, unity, and well-being.

— Peter Moustakerski
CEO, Family Office Exchange

Too many leaders feel compelled to set in stone the organization of their financial wealth or business ownership for all future generations — forgetting that what they put in place may disempower them, and that those generations may have entirely different needs and dreams.

This book reframes the entire conversation around estate planning; it calls on families and their advisors to define the human "why" before designing the legal "how."

— Christine Blondel
INSEAD, Wendel International Centre
for Family Enterprise

From Aristotle to Warren Buffett, many have observed that as hard as it is to create great financial wealth, it is even more difficult to pass it on well. In the face of this enduring challenge, the authors offer not only great experience and creativity, but above all the empathy and hope that are key to ensuring that good fortune truly enhances the lives of family members and their communities.

— Susan Massenzio, PhD
and Keith Whitaker, PhD
Wise Counsel Research

For families who value harmony, cultivate learning, and seek family flourishing the authors share their philosophy coupled with practical wisdom in this truly compelling work.

— Christian Stewart
Founder, Family Legacy Asia

The authors reveal how the real work of a flourishing family happens not in the estate plan but in living the culture that makes the plan work: the relationships, values, and quality of care that passes from one generation to the next. This book invites families and their advisors into that deeper conversation. It arrives at the right moment.

— Matt Wesley
Founder, Ascend Family Advisory

A unique and concise owner's guide to building the groundwork for family flourishing. The authors convey why a learning culture is a cornerstone, how to enrich the lives of beneficiaries, and what actions can be taken to move the family forward. Key concepts and important questions throughout provide a family roadmap to implementing their philosophy.

— Sara Hamilton
Founder, Family Office Exchange

The authors remind us that a life well-lived demands a much broader focus—encouraging readers to look beyond financial capital to factors that contribute to family well-being and a sense of individual purpose. Bravo to Hughes, Duke and Allred for underscoring the complexity of what it means to truly "do well."

— Madeline Levine, PhD
Author of *The Price of Privilege*,
Teach Your Children Well and *Ready or Not*

The stunning amount of wisdom, expertise, and empathy in this book will ensure wealth and well-being is sustained across generations. A must-read for families and their advisors.

— Meg Jay, PhD
Author of *The Defining Decade* and
The Twentysomething Treatment

This book reminds us that trusts and estate plans ultimately succeed or fail based not merely on the preservation of assets, but on whether they enhance the relationships of the human beings they serve.

— John A. Warnick, J.D.
Founder, Purposeful Planning Institute

Brilliant insights from some of the wisest minds on how to reclaim your legacy while "living within the plans" created by advisors. A must-read for family members navigating the complexity of living with trusts.

— Holly Isdale
CEO, Single Family Office

Family Flourishing

Family Flourishing

The True Meaning of Wealth

Reimagining Estate Planning,
Trust Administration, and Family Culture,
in Service of Generational Well-Being

JAMES E. HUGHES JR.
MARY K. DUKE
STACY L. ALLRED

James E. Hughes, Jr.
FOUNDATION
Publishing

James E. Hughes Jr. Foundation Publishing is part of the James E. Hughes Jr. Foundation. It furthers the mission of the Foundation to advance the field of family governance and generational well-being.

Published in the United States of America by James E. Hughes Jr. Publishing 2000 Morris Avenue, Suite 1300, Birmingham, Alabama, 35203

Library of Congress Cataloging-in-Publication Data:
Names: James E. Hughes Jr., author. | Mary K. Duke, author. | Stacy L. Allred, author. |

Title: Family Flourishing: The True Meaning of Wealth
Identifiers: ISBN 979-8-9886691-9-7 (hardback) |
ISBN 979-8-951068-99-6 (paperback) |
ISBN 979-8-951068-00-2 (epub) |
ISBN 979-8-951068-01-9 (audio)

Subjects: Trusts and trustees. | Beneficiaries. | Estate Planning. | Intergenerational relations. | Inheritance and succession. | Families—Economic aspects| Social capital (Sociology).| Values.

Dedication

To our loving families, where our own practice of flourishing begins and is renewed each day.

To the families for whom this book is offered, engaged in the intentional and ongoing work of creating the conditions in which flourishing can take root.

And to the advisors who accompany them, called to counsel with insight, intellectual humility, and care for the whole of a family's well-being.

Disclaimer

This book offers general perspectives on family wealth, estate planning, and trust administration. It is not a substitute for personalized legal, tax, or financial advice. Families should consult their own professional advisors regarding their specific circumstances before making decisions related to estate planning, trusts, governance, or family wealth structures. The authors and publisher disclaim any liability arising from reliance on the information contained herein.

Who this book is for:

- Individuals reviewing or preparing their estate plan who are seeking a more meaningful process while having a more humane impact on their descendants

- Individuals who are living with trusts—as beneficiaries of legal structures created by others

- Family members who are navigating the challenges and opportunities of significant financial wealth who seek to embrace a culture of care that can be sustained for generations

- The dedicated advisors who serve these individuals and their families

Contents

Chapter 3

Chapter 4

Chapter 5

Well-Being Lexicon

References

Acknowledgments

A book like this is never the work of its authors alone. It is shaped by conversations, communities, questions, encouragement, and the generosity of many people along the way. With three authors and wide circles of supporters, we know that any attempt to name everyone would inevitably leave someone out. So, we offer thanks with deep gratitude to all who have helped bring this work into being.

We are deeply grateful to Holly Isdale, Dennis Jaffe, Scott Peppet, Christian Stewart, Matt Wesley, and Keith Whittaker who generously read our manuscript before publication. Their thoughtful and candid feedback was immensely useful, and their insights and recommendations truly elevated the end product.

We offer our sincerest thanks to Catherine Rollhaus, executive director of the James E. Hughes Jr. Foundation, our publisher. Catherine has been, in every meaningful sense, a fourth partner in this process. She has helped guide our work with a keen eye, steady wisdom, and a wonderful sense of humor that eased the way through many challenges.

And for guiding us through the learning journey of creating this book, our heartfelt thanks to David Goetz, Melissa Parks, and Kirsten Tangeros and the team at Journey Sixty6.

Finally, Stacy and Mary want to express their deepest appreciation to Jay who is a dear friend and mentor, generous teacher, and one of the great visionaries of our field whose extraordinary generosity of spirit continues to shape its future. Your influence is felt deeply in the lives of so many fellow sojourners, as you invite us all to explore the big questions with courage, humility, and care.

And Jay would like to thank Jackie who *"put her arm through mine..."*

Preamble

In the last century, popular culture has eviscerated the word *wealth* by narrowing its meaning to money. The history of the word is much more holistic—and human.

Wealth originated from the word *weal*, which can be traced to an Old Saxon adverb, *wela*, meaning "well."[1] Its early meaning was rooted in well-being or welfare, not financial or material possessions.[2] This more life-giving meaning echoes Aristotle's concept of *eudaimonia*, often translated as "flourishing" or "the good life." Aristotle celebrated the virtuous life—fulfilling one's potential and contributing to the greater good.[3] He also taught that the family is the building block of society. We believe that a flourishing society begins with flourishing families.[4]

The true meaning of wealth is "well-being."

Revisiting wealth as well-being gives families a fresh lens through which to reimagine their legacy: one that supports the health, happiness, and harmony of all family members and the wider communities in which they live. Financial capital can and should serve in supporting these aims; it should not become the aim itself.

Throughout this book, when we use the word *wealth*, we mean well-being in this broader, older sense. When we refer to financial or economic wealth, we will say so.

We invite you to join us in changing the way we think and speak about wealth.

Chapter One

The Human Impact of Inheritance

Bridge or Barrier to Flourishing?

Meet Maddie

MADDIE MET OMAR in a jazz dance class her junior year in college. Soon after, they fell in love. Three years later, Omar proposed, and Maddie's parents were deeply unsettled. They loved their daughter and had imagined a very different future for her. They seemed to see Omar more through the lens of what made him unfamiliar than through the qualities Maddie loved.

Maddie wasn't entirely surprised by her parents' response. In their eyes, Omar was the construction contractor who had overseen the renovation at the studio where Maddie danced—he was not a college classmate, not someone from their world, and not what they had expected. Maddie says she wasn't in denial about her upbringing of privilege—the chauffeured school pickups; beautiful homes in exotic locations; a plane to shuttle the family between them; the wardrobes and waitstaff at each; the yacht; and an endless parade of toys and adventures to ensure no wisp of boredom ever wafted near the family.

She was not naïve. Or so she thought.

It was the meeting, held before the discussion of her prenuptial agreement with Omar, that awakened her to the nature of her family's economic success. Maddie was asked to attend a meeting at the family office—without Omar. It was her first-ever briefing with her family's attorneys. Maddie now calls it "The Great Reveal." The meeting lifted the veil on a world that she knew existed in some abstract sense, but she had been blissfully unaware of its complexity and details. In about 90 minutes, she learned just how much her family's estate was worth and was taken aback by how many strings were attached and how little she had access to or control over. Suddenly her future felt different.

The attorney repeatedly said, in various ways, "Now, Maddie, this conversation is meant to create clarity for you and give you a sense of security." Maddie left the meeting feeling newly insecure and with little clarity. The conversation seemed impersonal, almost clandestine.

The days following, Maddie grew more and more agitated. Her older sister, Ellie, who had "married up," becoming the wife of a rich scion from a high-profile family in their hometown, had not been required to have a prenup. Maddie's perception of this disparity in how her parents treated her and Omar created a rift in the family. It raised a lot of questions. She began to reflect on why her parents had hassled her over her living expenses as a dancer in college when these trust funds were sitting in the background. Her parents and their lawyers clearly saw Omar as a threat to the family's money. Was it because he didn't have a college degree? Or maybe it was because Omar was from a different country and raised in a different religion?

Maddie had mixed emotions. She felt grateful for the abundance that her family had provided her. But she was also confused, as the reveal opened a whole new set of questions and concerns, as well as potential issues with Omar. Deep tensions and divisions had long shaped her family, but as Maddie gained a clearer understanding of her grandfather's estate plan, she began to see how many of these fractures traced back to its provisions. Could he have ever imagined that his well-intended choices would deform the very family he had hoped to protect?

The impact of inheriting significant money can push individuals into extremes—either retreating into passivity or engaging in destructive conflict. But more often, it sows confusion, resentment, and discord as family members struggle under the weight of expectations. The Cornell Family Estrangement and Reconciliation Project[5] found that roughly 27 percent of Americans, 18 or older, are estranged from one or more family members. Money and inheritance rank as one of the top causes.[6] Maddie was on a path to joining one of the most painful life experiences: family cutoff.

Maddie's awakening is not unique among the second, third, and fourth generations of monied families. An apt metaphor for her experience is "a meteor event," a sudden impact that can ripple throughout a person's life for years to come.[7] It's clear there was little preparation for this initial "reveal" of the financial capital held for her benefit. Her family likely followed the pattern of the prior generation, keeping the financial assets cloaked in secrecy to maintain confidentiality until descendants were older.

Although a great estate plan is a critical element, it is just the starting point.

In this book, we argue that the true meaning of wealth is not money alone, but well-being, and that financial capital serves families best when it is designed, administered, and lived in ways that strengthen human, intellectual, social, and spiritual flourishing. Your family's legacy can be a gift of love that enhances the lives of your entire family—now and for future generations.

To secure this flourishing future, however, requires more than signing an estate plan. Estate plans and trusts are never merely technical structures; they shape identity, relationships, responsibility, and belonging. Although a great estate plan is a critical element, it is just the starting point. The provisions of that plan must be designed to support the family's flourishing across generations. And beyond the legal planning and subsequent trust administration, the most decisive aspect of a flourishing family is a flourishing culture: a family living its values, supporting the developmental journeys of its members, and supporting and engaging with the community in which it lives.

In this book, we invite families and their advisors to move beyond protection and tax efficiency alone toward a more qualitative approach anchored in three elements:

- Crafting a qualitative and humane estate plan, with control and flexibility in balance and financial capital as a gift of love in service to human, intellectual, social, and spiritual flourishing (Chapter 2);

- Building a trustee-beneficiary relationship where beneficiaries can enjoy a qualitative experience that supports their development individually and as a family (Chapter 3); and

- Activating the ways a family can foster a culture of care, for each other and community, that is carried from one generation to the next (Chapters 4 and 5).

These, we argue, are the elements critical to long-term family flourishing.

The life enhancement we envision means *every* member of your family is flourishing and, as Aristotle would say, living to his or her potential. This is why our definition of wealth must expand beyond mere financial capital to encompass true well-being. This starts with providing support for the qualitative well-being of all family members and the family itself. This is how your family can flourish across generations.

Preparing for the Meteor

Across the world, a vast transfer of economic wealth is in its early stages, driven by two key factors: the unprecedented global explosion of financial capital following World War II and the aging of the generations who hold it. This shift of financial capital to younger generations will result in an unprecedented number of "meteors" hitting families over the next several decades. The magnitude of this financial wealth transfer underscores the need for families and their advisors to ensure these transitions are guided by spirit and love—transforming them into meaningful gifts that enrich family members' lives and positively impact their communities.[8]

A rich family isn't necessarily a wealthy family.

We liken the effect of this great financial capital transfer to that of a meteor.[9] Intuitively, the first thought of a large inheritance is that it is some kind of bonanza, but for many family members, the experience (like Maddie's in her attorney's office), can feel, at least initially, emotional and overwhelming. That is, the money may feel more like a burden than a blessing.

An inheritance or gift of great magnitude—what we call the meteor—often arrives without warning, and often without context. It can disrupt the lives of beneficiaries who may be unprepared. This type of soulless transfer can quickly come to feel like an obligation. There are accounts to open, professionals to consult, people to appease, and responsibilities to shoulder—each step potentially creating a sense of disconnect rather than empowerment.

Of course, Maddie's meteor experience is not true for

all families, and with some focused effort it doesn't need to be true for your family.

Meteor-Proof: Families Built for Flourishing

Not every individual or family is thrown off course upon receiving financial assets.

Some beneficiaries, whether intuitively or with guidance, find a healthy equilibrium that allows them to integrate financial assets into their lives to fuel well-being. The key to success is laying the groundwork of preparation before the meteor hits. This involves a combination of love, support, and understanding—balanced with accountability, responsibility, healthy boundaries, and high expectations. For some families, this preparation is deeply embedded in the family culture. Nicoli's family is an example of this.

Nicoli is the grandson of a founder of a successful family business in Denmark. From a young age, Nicoli and his cousins attended family meetings, went on field trips to the various sites of their family businesses, and had an ongoing dialogue about what it meant to be a steward of a family-owned business. Nicoli and his family actively volunteered in their community, attended "financial boot camps," and organized a cohort of cousins who worked with family advisors to learn how to invest together.

Nicoli's parents supported him over the years as he developed, and his life's purpose evolved; they also held high expectations for him. When Nicoli came of age and fully grasped the magnitude of the family's financial

How Ready are you for the Meteor?

Integrating the Meteor				
Readiness	LOW **Shock & Scramble**	MODERATE **Finding a Footing**	HIGH **Resilience in Progress**	EXCEPTIONAL **Turn Impact into Momentum**
	Higher readiness before impact results in gentler impact.			

Impact	MAJOR	MODERATE	MINOR	GENTLE
Characteristics	• Sudden, disruptive, overwhelming. • Emotional and relational strain. • Lack of clarity on purpose, role, and responsibilities. • Asks: Why is this happening to me?	• Anticipated, with significant anxiety. • Mixed emotional reactions. • Partial clarity and alignment. • Asks: Why is this happening for me?	• Strong alignment with values and goals. • Defines roles. • Working on skill development. • Absorbs meteor.	• Aligned with purpose. • Generative: ability to work through challenges and optimize. • Acceptance; integrates meteor.
Action	• Build a foundational level of acceptance and understanding in this new reality. • Commit to building a support system and beginning the work.	• Explore what this means. • Develop plan to prepare. • Learn from others navigating similar situations. • Encourage collaborative, holistic planning.	• Celebrate the gift's meaning and potential. • Develop a plan for learning, growth, and development.	• Ongoing communication, reflection of values and meaning. • Elevated skill building, from learning to development.

assets, he still felt the weight of responsibility but also felt equipped to navigate the journey. Nicoli stood on solid ground as the meteor arrived. Prepared for the impact, he knew who he was, what he was capable of, and what really mattered.

This coming wave of asset transfers around the world is likely to result in a continuum of experiences (see the "Burnout to Flourishing" graphic). On the left, there will likely be "burnout" among families who will be hit by the meteor and never experience the true meaning of the word *wealth* as well-being. On the opposite end of the spectrum is "flourishing," which is our vision for your family. In between are various states, such as "struggling," "surviving," and "thriving"—which is where many families will fall. Money is easy to measure and track, but just

From Burnout to Flourishing

because it is measurable does not mean it is the most important asset of the family. A rich family isn't necessarily a wealthy family, if they aren't prepared for the meteor. Without a thoughtful, balanced, or holistic approach, financial capital that was meant to enhance the lives of family members may instead create barriers to personal fulfillment and familial harmony.

Bridge to the Future

When money enters a family system, drama can intensify. Money often introduces a complex set of emotional and psychological challenges.

In our work with families, we hear of the rising generation experiencing a fear of messing things up or guilt for not having "earned" the money they inherited. Some of these emerging adults feel as if they don't measure up, and they struggle to get out of the long shadow that the outsized success of preceding generations creates. Others seem to have a sense of entitlement to the money and the opportunities it can open, which can erode motivation and relationships. Within a monied family, a narrow definition of "wealth as financial assets" can become an instrument of discord rather than harmony, fostering confusion, entitlement, and resentment.

Increasingly, a small but mighty cohort of advisors and firms are focusing on the broader, true meaning of wealth.

For Maddie to flourish, she will need to find her voice and agency within the complexity of the legal structures that her grandfather had set up for the family. That comes with opportunities, responsibilities, and challenges. That means, first and foremost, she will need to accept her family's protectiveness while cultivating her growth-oriented mindset: Her attorneys had presented her with a "plan" originally drafted with a "protector mindset," focused on protecting the financial assets from creditors and taxes. Now, she must shift her thinking to our fuller definition of wealth as well-being.

That raises important questions. How can Maddie move beyond feeling controlled by the rules and secrecy and the quantitative, protective approach of her family's financial assets? How can she appreciate the benefits of the structure and begin thinking about the human and cultural aspects of what she has been given?

Many inheritors find themselves navigating a system designed primarily to protect and perpetuate financial capital, often at the expense of personal agency and broader well-being. Consider the vast number of companies that comprise the "wealth" management industry serving wealthy families. In our experience, most are still primarily focused on financial capital, which is only one of the five capitals of family wealth.[10] These advisors serve primarily to protect assets; they are not equipped to nurture the well-being of families.

Increasingly, a small but mighty cohort of advisors and firms are focusing on the broader, true meaning of wealth, addressing the human, intellectual, social, and spiritual capital of families in addition to managing the financial capital. For the Maddies of the future to flourish, the number of qualitative advisors needs to expand to serve the burgeoning number of families being hit by these meteoric asset transfers.

Bucking the Status Quo for What Can Be

No doubt, Maddie's grandparents thought they were doing the right thing when they originally sat down decades ago with their attorney to draft the documents for their family's trust. Most family elders who organize their affairs do not intend for their descendants to feel trapped by rigid legal structures. Most likely they also inadvertently conflated the word *wealth* with financial assets. And their advisors drafted documents that reflected that narrow thinking.

The challenge is that traditional trusts don't anticipate the future needs of family members, or the broader society 20 years into the future, much less a century. Perpetual trusts are designed to last forever, benefiting future generations over centuries. Trusts shield assets from creditors, lawsuits, and divorce claims. But they fail to consider the evolving needs of future generations. Trusts, by design, may not account for well-being, as they attempt to lock in decisions for an indefinite future. Because their qualitative needs were under-considered at the creation of the estate plan, inheritors in future generations, like Maddie, may experience the transfer of financial assets as disruptive.

At the beginning of the chapter, we introduced the idea that for descendants to experience a trust as a gift of love, a trust creator must think and act differently about wealth. The greatest asset on a family's balance sheet is the family itself—its members, their relationships, and their contributions. A family will need to counterbalance the rigid, quantitative aspects of typical estate planning with a focus on life enhancement for beneficiaries and a culture of care.

This redefining of wealth requires courage—the courage to question old narratives, redefine success, and cultivate a culture of trust and resilience within your family. Families that flourish across generations are those willing to have courageous conversations, address tensions head on, and make intentional choices that reflect their desires for a more holistic view of *wealth:* wealth as well-being. You may need to be the one that pushes your drafting attorney to take this shift seriously.

Readers may look for a model to follow or a checklist to complete. We have resisted that impulse, not because structure lacks value (we offer principles and themes throughout), but because flourishing cannot be standardized. We don't offer a formula to implement, but a way of seeing that each family must interpret and live for itself.

The greatest asset on a family's balance sheet is the family itself.

This book aims to provide practical wisdom and actionable tools to help you navigate the complexities of growing real wealth—human, intellectual, social, spiritual, and financial capital. In the next chapter, we'll focus on what a "qualitative estate plan" could look like for your family. To achieve this shift, families must widen the lens—and look beyond immediate financial concerns to examine the broader system that influences their well-being.

Have You Considered…

- ❍ If a significant transfer of financial wealth arrived in your family tomorrow, what feelings would you anticipate having—excitement, anxiety, relief, dread? What does your reaction tell you?

- ❍ Think of the most "meteor-proof" person you know—someone who integrated good fortune into a life well-lived. What made them that way?

- ❍ What's one unspoken rule about money in your family that everyone knows but no one says out loud? Is it helpful? Or an impediment?

- ❍ Where in your family's current planning is the emphasis more on *protecting* than *preparing*? Is that the balance you'd choose?

- ❍ If your inheritance came with a handwritten note from the person who created it, what would you most hope it said?

From Insight to Action: What is your key takeaway?

Chapter Two

A Qualitative Estate Plan

Drafting an Estate Plan with Both Love and Structure

***Authors' Note**: This chapter is addressed primarily to family members who are engaged in the process of creating or revising their estate plan, and to the advisors who serve them. The principles presented are meant to guide reflection and dialogue; each family's estate planning and trust decisions should ultimately be shaped in consultation with advisors who understand the family's particular circumstances.*

Maddie, Continued: The Quest for Clarity

AS THE INITIAL SHOCK of learning about the trust began to settle, Maddie did what she had always done when faced with something unfamiliar. She dug in and worked to understand it. She assumed that if she asked the right questions, clarity would follow.

She reached out to the estate planning firm that had drafted her grandfather's will years earlier. The firm was still respected, still busy. Yet almost no one there had known her grandfather personally. After some searching, she learned that the associate who had worked most closely on the plan early in his career was now a retired partner. With some effort, the family arranged a conversation.

Maddie entered that conversation hopeful. The retired lawyer was kind and generous with his time. He could explain why certain provisions had been common at the time, what risks her grandfather had likely been concerned about, and how the law had changed since then. What he could not do was speak with confidence about what her grandfather had hoped life with the trust would feel like, or how relationships within the family were meant to unfold.

As she listened, Maddie noticed a gap. The documents were precise, carefully drafted, and technically sound. The intentions behind them, however, felt remote and unclear. She realized that the estate plan had been created at a single point in time but was now being asked to carry meaning across generations and circumstances that its creators could not have fully imagined.

Maddie did not leave the conversation angry or disappointed. Instead, she left disoriented. She had assumed that understanding the plan would help her understand her place within it. What she encountered instead was a system well equipped to describe structure, but less able to offer her guidance about finding purpose, belonging, or an understanding of how a real family made up of different and evolving individuals might live well together inside it.

Of course, technical rigor in estate planning for financially successful families is critical. In fact, it is expected and assumed. Technical excellence in estate planning is a deeply honed practice area, and many expert technicians embody that standard in the trust and estate legal field.

However, the qualitative estate planning model that we are arguing for starts with the why, not just the how. Rather than beginning your planning process with tax strategies and asset protection, you will want to ask the deeper question: How will this plan serve the well-being of my family—today and in the future?

As highly skilled as most estate attorneys are, they typically are not trained to guide families through this type of self-reflection. They are unlikely to explore the inevitable, cultural impact of the estate plan on your family members. As a result, the emotional, relational, and cultural effect a plan may have on the well-being of future generations remains, in most cases, largely unexamined.

When estate plans don't address these deeper dynamics, the consequences often show up in subtle but disruptive ways. A beneficiary may feel a compromised sense of autonomy, with simmering resentment due to a lack of control over trust assets. Another might lose motivation to pursue work or a career, believing that earning a salary is financially irrelevant. Some families experience tensions in family relationships arising out of the interdependencies the plan imposes. For example, resentment may surface when siblings serve as each other's trustees or when family members are beneficiaries of a single trust (referred to as a pot trust), in which assets are held collectively and one beneficiary may consume the assets faster, leaving others with less.

This is why getting the drafting right is mission critical: The plan you and your estate counsel craft over a period of months can create structures that your family will be living with for generations. (In the case of perpetual trusts, theoretically, forever![11]) It takes a special approach to ensure the drafting is more than a legal exercise. Only when your plan has expanded to provide for the qualitative needs of the family can it create the setting for your family to flourish for generations. Done well, it can be an act of love, vision, and courage. It should reflect the soul of the family, not just its balance sheet.

Only when your plan has expanded to provide for the qualitative needs of the family can it create the setting for your family to flourish for generations.

Trust Attorney as Playwright

If your intent in creating an estate plan is to ensure your assets enhance the lives of your beneficiaries, we encourage you to find an estate planning attorney who is an exceptional technician and, just as important, is comfortable crafting something more than a document to protect your family's financial capital. Someone more like a playwright.

A Note to Families New to Trusts & Sophisticated Estate Planning

Families often arrive at significant financial capital in different ways. Some family members grow up with substantial resources and never know another economic experience. They are, in a sense, natives to wealth.[12] Others encounter significant financial capital later in life, through entrepreneurship, professional success, or inheritance. These families and individuals can be thought of as immigrants to wealth, learning new norms, language, and expectations as they go.

We find this distinction equally helpful when thinking about trusts and sophisticated estate planning.

Over the past several decades, the rapid global expansion of economic wealth is leading many families to encounter trusts for the first time. In many cases, the generation that created the capital is also the generation now designing estate plans that may shape family life for decades, or even centuries, to come. For families who have not previously lived with trusts, it can be difficult to anticipate how these structures will be experienced by children, grandchildren, and future generations.

If your family is new to financial wealth, new to trusts, or both, we encourage you to slow down the process. Take time to consider not only what you are trying to protect, but how the structures you create may be "lived in" by your descendants. Estate plans are typically drafted at a single moment in time, yet their effects unfold across many lives and changing circumstances.

Most advisors are trained to focus on legal, tax, and technical excellence, and that expertise is essential. At the same time, the long-term human implications of trusts are not always fully explored in the drafting process. This book is an invitation to widen that lens, to think about culture alongside structure, and to consider how learning, care, and relationship can be supported over time.

Think of the earliest playwrights, the Greeks, from whom we have the classical definitions of tragedy and comedy. In dramatic terms, a tragedy ends with all the main characters dead, having failed in their attempt to navigate the play's central conflict. In terms of a family, a tragedy looks like members roiled in conflict or, more often, simply drifting into disconnection, their sense of agency and shared purpose unraveling; in other words, the family dies. On the other hand, a dramatic comedy ends with its characters standing on their proverbial feet, having navigated the story's crisis, ready and equipped to move forward.

In this sense, the writing of an estate plan is the crafting of a script that has the potential to hold great sway over your family for generations. Think of your family members as the players in this play being written. Are you considering what they will need to learn for their roles? Are you creating opportunities for rehearsals? Are they benefiting from wise direction so they can embrace their role as beneficiary, interpret the role as their own, and evolve from scripted performance to confident improvisation?

Ask yourself, "Can my family 'play' in the play I am creating with my attorney?"

A New Partnership Between Trust Creator and Drafting Attorney

You and your drafting attorney have enormous power over whether your family lives in a comedy or a tragedy. How your family's initial trust is drafted can reverberate for generations. Too often, though, family members find

Potential Consequences of a Plan Narrowly Focused on Protection		
Compromised Sense of Autonomy	**Stymied Personal Productivity**	**Complicated Relationships**
Resentment over the lack of control over trust assets.	Interest in pursuing work eroded because pay feels largely irrelevant.	Tensions arising out of imposed interdependencies, such as siblings serving as each other's trustees or sharing assets, like a family vacation home.
Sense of dependency on trust distributions.	Guilt over choice of career or lifestyle—where the trust document sets expectations or specifies rewards for specific behaviors, like work, marriage, or religion.	Beneficiaries race to consume shared assets before they are gone or consumed by other beneficiaries.
Lack of flexibility to support current needs.	Mandated distributions that remove the necessity to work, impacting motivation for a beneficiary who hasn't yet developed purpose.	Stress on marriages where only one spouse has access to significant trust funds. This can be especially hard on couples where the wife is the beneficiary of significant assets.[13]

they can't "play" in the play that has been scripted for them. The structure is rigid, the roles unfamiliar, and the outcome feels inevitable—more tragedy than comedy.

When planning begins with a narrow definition of wealth—as just the material or financial assets—attorneys (the playwrights) approach their drafting with a "protector mindset."[14] The focus is solely on protecting the financial assets from creditors and taxes at all costs. These goals are important, but when balanced with a broader definition of well-being, the result is a plan that truly will elevate your family members.

We encourage you to engage in a partnership with your estate attorney to create a play (that is, an estate plan) that empowers family members to improvise, grow, and stay connected, rather than locking them into a rigid performance. Your estate plan can create the circumstances for family members to move toward flourishing on the continuum—and away from languishing.

When your estate plan is done, ask yourself, "Can my family live in this plan, and does it offer the conditions for flourishing?"

If you can answer with a resounding yes, you've done more than protect assets—you've written a future your family can grow into.

Key Attributes of a Qualitative Estate Plan

A qualitative estate plan does not emerge by accident. It reflects a deliberate shift in focus—from legal documents alone to the lives those documents will shape. In our experience, three attributes consistently distinguish estate plans that support family flourishing from those that merely transfer assets. They are not technical innovations, but expressions of the intention of life enhancement: making the plan personal, building in adaptability, and designing the structure to support the growth of human capital.

We expand on each of these below.

Make Your Estate Plan Personal

Inheritance is an emotional and often difficult experience under the best of circumstances. In the movies, an inheritor is called into the dark and somber lawyer's office for the "reading of the will" by someone they've never met and have no affinity with. The moment is formal, impersonal, and strangely detached from the life that preceded it. In real life, it is not much better. Is that what you want for your heirs? Instead, consider making your estate plan's language—at least its preamble—more approachable and personal. This can have a number of benefits: Primarily, it can ease the emotional impact of your passing, when the time comes, and put your inheritors at ease so they are better able to engage in discussion with your representatives. A thoughtful preamble will better reflect you personally, rather than a dusty old law book.

Our dear friend and estate planning attorney, John A. Warnick, founded the Purposeful Planning Institute out of his passion for transforming the estate planning experience to be more qualitative—and purposeful. He often reminds clients, "We must make sure the illuminating light of our vision and heartfelt purposes is captured in our Purposeful Plan. Otherwise, it could be virtually anyone's plan."

With typical drafting, Warnick points out, if the first page and the last page are torn off a trust deed, it can be impossible to identify the trust creator behind the deed. Among many things, he recommends naming your trust something truly meaningful to you, the trust creator.

We've seen this advice at work in a family meeting where the planning attorney reviewed a carefully crafted flowchart showing the eight trusts in the family's estate plan. The family members had been asked in advance to think of a tagline for each of the eight trusts based on the purpose that each trust served.

A qualitative plan is one that is personal, has a clearly stated intent to enhance the lives of the beneficiaries, has flexibility, and provides for the well-being of its beneficiaries.

At first the family leaders felt this was an unnecessary distraction. The nuts and bolts of each trust were clear upon reading each trust deed. But the discussion that followed added rich color and texture to the purpose of each trust. As the family developed a tagline for each trust, conversations were filled with laughter, questions, and insights. Most of all, the dialogue and memorable taglines resulted in clarity on the core purpose of each trust that would stick well into the future. This is just one element of building a level of clarity and understanding of the trusts for each family member.

When you name the trust, you claim authorship, becoming "co-playwright" in your unfolding family story. This can inspire family understanding of the trust and spark a desire to live up to its intent: a more hopeful path to a flourishing future.

Declare Your Intent

We encourage you, if you do nothing else, to add this simple language at the beginning of your trust, clearly establishing your overall intention: "This trust is a gift of love intended to enhance the lives of the beneficiaries."

It is the easiest and least controversial language to add.

More importantly, it mandates that the trustee engages deeply with the beneficiaries to assess how the trust can best support the flourishing of individual family members and the family as a whole. This preamble sets the tone for the entire trust. It becomes a mission statement for generations. These words empower (actually require!) the trustee to consider each beneficiary and to develop an understanding of what enhancement means to those individuals. It invites the trustee to step beyond the administrative and investment roles and into an enduring relationship with the beneficiaries—one grounded in understanding of what well-being looks like for each and how the trust can enhance each life journey.

Further Clarify Your Intentions: Use Side Letters to Add Meaning and Detail

Beyond this sentence in the preamble, you can also give your trustee a fuller picture of your intent: your hopes for how you would like your structure to enhance the lives of your descendants.

One wealth creator put a tremendous amount of time and effort into his estate plan when he realized that something was lacking. As he put it, "The cover letter to my estate plan was missing!" At his attorney's urging, he drafted two separate, but complementary, letters: a letter of wishes to his trustee and a legacy letter (also called a love letter, or ethical will[15]) to his family.

He put as much care into the letters as he put into the estate plan. He and his wife shared both of these letters with their adult children. While the letter of wishes was technically to the trustee, it would impact family members—so they felt transparency was essential. That openness, coupled with an ongoing dialogue, became a meaningful and important step in fostering understanding and awareness of the plan among their children—their descendants.

Letters of Wishes

If you ask trustees what makes a big difference as they carry out their duties, you will frequently hear, "a letter of wishes." Yet only a small percentage of trust creators actually write these.

It's important to consider the trustee's ability to carry out your wishes.

A letter of wishes[16] is a side letter to your trustee and is written at the same time as your estate plan. It sits alongside the trust deed to provide your trustee with a deeper understanding of your intent for the trust. A letter of wishes is precatory, meaning not legally binding and cannot change the terms of the trust document. While a letter of wishes is technically for your trustee, you can proactively share it with your family as an opportunity to spark dialogue and create clarity among all members. It's important to consider the trustee's ability to carry out your wishes and provision for additional support if needed (such as a special advisor to help with family dynamics or conflict).

A letter of wishes may set out how trustees will be evaluated and what their priorities should be. Beyond that, it can express the values and virtues most important to the trust creator. It can define terms like "education" and "spending" in ways that reflect the trust creator's intentions. These definitions help encourage specific values or behaviors (without being proscriptive), clarify intended uses of funds, and convey the spirit behind distributions.

Legacy Letters

It's not just the trustees who value a letter with guidance from the trust creator. Time and time again, we have stepped into family systems where family members long for a window into their ancestor's perspective and wish for a way to tap into their wisdom.

One family hired a historian to create a "postmortem" legacy letter, a project that required culling through journals and board meeting minutes as well as interviewing people who knew their ancestor. How much more powerful would it have been if the wealth creator had taken the time to create this letter while the opportunity existed?

A legacy letter can be written at any time and changed or added to over the years. You can write one to each person, or to the family as a whole. You can even speak to those family members yet to be born or married in. This is where your values can truly shine through in the form of "guidelights."[17] Share what has shaped you, along with your wishes and even regrets. Set out the principles that matter to you. You can even include books and poems that have impacted you. Importantly, you can explain the meaning behind certain items you have left to someone. Sharing the story can transform a mere gift into a priceless and appreciated treasure.[18]

Provide a Way for the Structure to Adapt—Creating a Flexible Plan

It is natural to want to set out some guidelines or restrictions for how descendants will use estate assets in the future. However, one of the greatest challenges of estate planning is this: no document drafted today can possibly anticipate or solve for all the needs and complexities of future generations. One family patriarch created a trust with *one hundred* (really!) stipulations as to what family members had to do to qualify for distributions.

Some of his restrictions had to do with religion—for example, whom the children could marry. There were restrictions on how far they could live from the family estate and also requirements on how and when each could actually use the money. The details were excruciatingly precise.

It was so over the top that their family office executive joked that the list should be printed on the back of a T-shirt. (She was fired.) Sadly, the situation got even worse when the patriarch and his wife unexpectedly died in a tragic accident. One of their children—so overwhelmed by the restrictions and how they extinguished his autonomy—*opted out of the inheritance* entirely, leaving his siblings to share the entire estate. The trust, meant to protect and provide for the descendants, ultimately alienated one of them. All because the father sought to rigidly impose his values and views on his descendants.

An estate plan that prescriptive can be a recipe for failure. It may lock in cultural views and stifle the very people the plan is meant to support. Its rigidity fails to account for how families grow and change—for shifting values, unexpected life paths, and the complexity of human relationships over time. Romantic poet Percy Bysshe Shelley's great poem "Ozymandias"[19] offers a sobering warning: The once-great king boasts, "Look on my works, ye Mighty, and despair!"—but nothing remains but a "colossal wreck" and "lone and level sands." In the same way, wealth creators who try to cement their influence too tightly through rigid planning may become like Ozymandias—believing their legacy will endure, only to leave "half sunk, a shattered visage" in the sand.

The antidote isn't more rules. It's more thoughtful design.

Provisions often enter the trust structure as a mechanism of control or a response to fear that the money will harm family members. During the drafting phase, families often voice a common concern: "I don't want the money to mess up our kids." (We address this question more deeply in chapter 4.) This desire to "get it right" for the next generation can also lead to excessive rigidity.

The antidote, though, isn't more rules. It's more thoughtful design.

A wealth creator asked us, "How can I structure my

estate plan in a way that balances the technical rigor my lawyer insists is required to ensure it is legally compliant with the ability for my plan to adapt to sensible shifts and unforeseen changes in my family?" This astute question gets to the heart of another key challenge—the tension between the legal (technical) and the human (emotional) aspects of estate planning.

These tensions cannot be resolved by choosing one over the other, but they instead present a challenge to dynamically balance the two.[20] This is the very essence of qualitative estate planning. It requires you and your planning attorney to move beyond either/or thinking and into the harder, braver work of both/and. Trusts enable families to flourish when they recognize and balance these natural tensions that exist within the family system—between autonomy and togetherness, tradition and innovation, and transparency and privacy. A well-crafted estate plan doesn't force a choice. It provides enough structure to carry the grantor's values and vision, yet is spacious enough to allow for interpretation, growth, and human judgment.

That's what demands courage: holding space for complexity when what people really want is control. Courage means trusting future generations to know what they will need. As Adam Kahane, a leading thinker in collaborative leadership, says, "When we pretend that … our challenges are simple rather than complex, we get stuck. If we want to get unstuck, we need to acknowledge our interdependence, cooperate, and feel our way forward. We need therefore to employ not only our power but also our love. If this sounds easy, it's not."[21] Courage means balancing power with love.

Drafting for Flexibility and Well-Being

Flexibility is not just a mindset or a way of thinking. It can be designed into the trust itself. There are concrete strategies that allow a trust to adapt over time while staying rooted in its original intent. Here are a few practical ways to infuse more flexibility into a trust as it is initially drafted:

- Balance clear rules with flexibility to adapt to a changing family and world.
- Create sufficient room for the trust deed and its administration to evolve, while still being enforceable.
- Provide flexibility—don't be too prescriptive, because circumstances change and challenges arise.
- Allow the trustee to use contemporary metrics for measures in the future.
- Avoid the urge to boil the ocean—focus on what has the most meaning or impact.

A Way Back Home

One of the biggest estate planning mistakes is creating an exclusion that leaves "no way back home." Once the trust creator has died, it is simply too late to explain or revise a provision that creates an emotional wound, whether intentionally or through misinterpretation. The family member who is injured must figure out how to rationalize what happened and find a way to move forward.

An example of a prescriptive clause is to require the

beneficiaries to adhere to a religious or political practice. When a trust hardwires moral judgment into its provisions, it removes the possibility of redemption.

The rigidity encoded in these trusts can carry permanent consequences. Instead of fostering relationship with a beneficiary as a unique and beloved person, trusts with exclusions impose moral judgments—leading to an individual being cut off and alienated. The family member may live forever under the shadow of that exclusion. That wound is not only public, but it becomes part of the lore of the family.

This type of provision also creates thorny questions. Who will be tasked to judge whether a family member is compliant? What remedy exists for an unfair determination?

A wise plan includes a way back: a chance to be seen, to grow, to rejoin the family.

The idea of redemption—of coming home again—is a universal theme in philosophy and all major religions and crosses all cultural lines. People can and do change. A well-written trust leaves room for someone to come back—to return home. Horrible things can happen in families—and families can heal from them and move on. A trust should never be the final word on a person's worth. A wise plan includes a way back: a chance to be seen, to grow, to rejoin the family. Without that, the trust becomes not a gift but a life sentence.

Ultimately, a flourishing family must ask an even deeper question: Will we be a welcoming family? We return to this theme in chapter 4, when we explore the cultural foundations that allow love, belonging, and renewal to endure across generations.

Focus on Growing Human Capital

A qualitative estate plan is not neutral about what it is trying to preserve.

If its sole objective is the protection and growth of financial capital, it may succeed in safeguarding assets while inadvertently weakening the very people those assets were meant to serve. A truly qualitative estate plan recognizes that the most important "assets" of any trust are not financial, but the human beings whose lives it touches.

To focus on growing human capital is to embed care for beneficiaries directly into the legal architecture of the plan. It means empowering trustees not merely to steward investment portfolios, but to steward people—to invest in their education, development, health, resilience, and capacity for contribution over time.[22]

This does not transform trustees into therapists or parents. It does, however, expand the lens through which success is measured. The question becomes not simply "Were the assets preserved?" but also "Were the lives of the beneficiaries enhanced?"

That shift in orientation changes drafting decisions in subtle but powerful ways.

Creating a Share for the Family

One practical way to reflect this orientation is to recognize that families are not only collections of individuals but living systems. For example, when dividing an estate among children, some families choose to create individual shares as well as a separate share dedicated to the family as a whole—a "well-being share." If there are four branches in the family, create a fifth share for the family.

Such a share establishes a pool of resources devoted to the shared life of the family: gatherings, education, conflict resolution support, shared philanthropic initiatives, or other activities that strengthen relationships across branches.

This approach becomes especially important as families grow and branches diverge in size. Without intentional design, tension can emerge between larger branches and smaller ones. A share set aside for the family signals that some resources are dedicated not to individual accumulation but to sustaining connection and cohesion.

The message is clear: The family itself matters.

Embedding Autonomy Rather Than Dependency

Human capital grows where autonomy is nurtured and respected.

Where possible, qualitative plans seek to maximize beneficiary agency rather than centralize control. This may include language to allow beneficiaries to take on increasing autonomy and responsibility as they mature and exhibit readiness. A few examples include:

- Using separate trusts for individual beneficiaries rather than large "pot" trusts that are shared by all and may create competition among beneficiaries racing to consume assets. These shared trusts are often opaque about how beneficiaries can participate, which can undermine their confidence in the system.

- Naming beneficiaries as their own trustees, when appropriate, or as co-trustees along with experienced fiduciaries.

- Allowing beneficiaries, within reasonable guardrails, to appoint and remove trustees.

These structures communicate confidence. They treat beneficiaries not as risks to be managed but as adults capable of stewardship over time. Autonomy does not eliminate accountability. It simply aligns responsibility with authority—an alignment that supports growth rather than resentment.

Considering More Lifetime Gifts

In an era of increasing longevity and expanding economic capital, it is worth asking whether all financial transfers should occur at death.

Holding assets until the end of life may inadvertently delay support until it is least impactful. For many families, there are moments in early adulthood—education, entrepreneurship, home formation, or family building—when financial support can have disproportionate positive effect.

Lifetime gifts, whether outright or in trust, allow resources to reach beneficiaries when they can best use them. They also allow the older generation to witness the impact of their generosity, to guide where appropriate, and to learn alongside the next generation.

This is not a call for imprudence. It is an invitation to reflect on timing. Capital deployed at the right moment can be developmental rather than merely distributive.

Avoiding the Illusion of Incentive Trusts

Few drafting devices reflect fear more clearly than the incentive trust.

An incentive trust attempts to engineer specific behaviors by tying distributions to accomplishments: earning degrees, maintaining employment, achieving certain income levels, or adhering to lifestyle requirements. While often well-intentioned, such provisions assume that financial reward is an effective motivator of complex human traits such as work ethic, responsibility, or integrity.

Research in behavioral science consistently suggests otherwise.[23] Financial incentives can influence simple, transactional tasks. They are far less effective at cultivating intrinsic motivation, resilience, creativity, or ethical character—the very attributes families hope to encourage. More importantly, highly prescriptive incentive provisions risk sending the unintended message that love and support are conditional upon performance.

A qualitative estate plan resists this temptation. It prefers flexibility, articulated values, and trusted discretion over rigid behavioral scripting. Applying these principles shapes how resources are distributed to individuals. Some families also choose to reflect their commitment to human capital at the governance level.

Establishing a Beneficiary Relations Committee

One way to embed care for beneficiaries directly into the architecture of a trust is to establish a beneficiary relations committee, sometimes structured as a distribution committee under the terms of the trust. While traditional trusts often concentrate distribution authority in a single trustee or corporate fiduciary, a well-designed committee can bring relational focus and developmental intent to that decision-making process.

At its best, a beneficiary relations committee is not simply a mechanism for approving or denying distributions. Its role is broader and more human. It exists to ensure that the trust enhances the lives of each beneficiary and that the administration of the trust remains aligned with the family's commitment to growing human capital.

Such a committee can help create an intentional space for engagement. Members may serve as mentors, helping beneficiaries understand the purpose of the trust, the responsibilities that accompany stewardship, and the opportunities available to them. They can support beneficiaries in learning how to reflect on their goals and make thoughtful requests, articulating how resources will be used in service of growth rather than consumption.

Importantly, this also requires helping beneficiaries learn what it means to be "accounted to" by a trustee. Trustees have fiduciary obligations that shape how and when they can act. A beneficiary relations committee can clarify those boundaries, reinforcing mutual respect between trustee and beneficiary. When beneficiaries understand the trustee's role and the principles guiding discretionary decisions, the relationship shifts from adversarial or transactional to collaborative and developmental.

Legally, such committees can be structured in a variety of ways, depending on jurisdiction and drafting approach. They may hold formal discretionary authority over distributions, operate in a directed trust framework alongside an administrative trustee, or serve in an advisory capacity or as a board committee of a private trust company. The technical design matters, but the deeper point remains the same: the committee exists to humanize the trust relationship and to ensure that financial capital serves the development of people.

Like any structure, a beneficiary relations committee will magnify the culture of the family that creates it. In families committed to learning, transparency, and mutual respect, it can become a powerful vehicle for mentoring and growth. In families unprepared for that work, it risks becoming another layer of governance without meaning. As with all qualitative planning, structure must follow intention. Emerging legal structures, such as the US Delaware Well-Being Trust, reflect a similar recognition at the statutory level—that well-being can be an explicit objective of trust design.

A Note on Emerging Structures: The Delaware Well-Being Trust

Recent innovations in trust law, including the US Delaware Well-Being Trust,[24] reflect an emerging recognition that trustees may have an explicit mandate to consider beneficiary well-being, not merely preservation of financial assets. (Notably, there are estate planning practitioners who have incorporated provisions supporting well-being language in their plans well before the more recent arrival of these new structures, but they are few and far between.)

While such structures are still developing, they underscore an important conceptual shift. Trust law itself is beginning to acknowledge what many families intuitively understand: that the purpose of a trust is not solely financial continuity, but human flourishing.

As with any legal innovation, the effectiveness of such structures depends on the clarity of intention and the culture surrounding them. No statute can create care where it does not exist. But well-designed structures can empower trustees to act in ways that align financial stewardship with human development.

An estate plan that grows human capital is not more

complicated. It is simply more intentional about what success truly means.

Do the Pre-Work with Your Family

It may be tempting to jump straight to the legal work of drafting an estate plan, but that's not where we recommend you begin. Doing foundational thinking before selecting a drafting attorney sets the stage for a more meaningful and aligned outcome. Before you engage your drafting attorney, consider engaging a guide to help you and your family identify your values, your perspective on the purpose of your financial capital, and your vision for flourishing as a family for generations to come. Your ideal planning team might include both an attorney and a specialist advisor[25]—someone to help articulate the human "why" before the legal "how."

Sometimes you can get both in a single attorney, but the reality is that attorneys are navigating immense technical complexity. Between tax mitigation, asset protection, and fiduciary liability, drafting modern trusts can feel like three-dimensional chess requiring strategic foresight at every step. In short, don't rely solely on your attorney to lead your purpose conversation. It's a big ask to expect someone consumed with legal precision to also draw out your family's deep story and intention.

A well-drafted trust begins long before pen meets paper. When families do the work—before the documents are drawn—to clarify what matters most, they give their plan meaning and their family the optimum environment to flourish.

A Note on Selecting Trustees and Successors

One of the hardest decisions of the estate planning process is naming the trustee. Yet the decision is larger than simply choosing someone you know and trust today. Consider that your trust is likely to exist for several generations. Even if it only lasts 20 years, it is very likely that the trustee named in your documents will need to be replaced. So beyond identifying your trustee today—spend time crafting guidance for the future decisions to be made.

- Make technical expertise your baseline.
- Consider the key duties of a trustee—duties of care, loyalty, and accountability. Ensure that your selected trustee can satisfy these duties while maintaining impartiality.
- Set out clear criteria in the form of attributes and competencies sought in trustees. This is more important than names—the trust is likely to last longer than people who are alive today. (See "Personal Attributes of a Qualitative Trustee" in chapter 3.)
- Consider what the trust holds. If it holds an operating company, real estate, or exotic assets, the trustees need this expertise!
- Establish a process for how to choose and replace trustees because there will likely be many trustees over the decades ahead.
- Ensure flexibility to adapt and evolve. The shelf life of an individual trustee is relatively short!
- Consider playing to strengths by having more than one trustee, combining a corporate or professional trustee with an extended family member or friend as co-trustee or protector. (Family and friends may know your family and have personal connection that helps support beneficiaries but are unlikely to have the expertise to manage the administration and oversee the financial assets in the trust. Corporate trustees have more expertise but are known for having a keen risk aversion and focus on avoiding liability, above nurturing the human capital of the family.)

The Best Plans

Every inheritor faces an integration problem. In the coming years, trillions of dollars will be set in motion through estate plans as part of the great wealth transfer. But this isn't merely economic intermediation—it's an emotional reckoning. A meteor is hitting families, and the real question is this: How will that impact integrate into the lives of the people it's meant to support?

That's where a qualitative plan makes all the difference.

A qualitative plan does more than manage money—it creates the conditions for family members to *live in the plan*, not feel constrained by it. It's flexible. Like a thoughtfully written script, it invites interpretation, encourages growth, and allows room for evolving roles. And it prepares heirs for the emotional and relational realities of inheritance. Without this kind of foresight, even the best-intended plan can become rigid and performative—more tragedy than comedy.

We have seen families who take this broader, qualitative approach to estate planning gain greater clarity, build stronger relationships, and create estate plans that remain resilient as lives and circumstances change. At their best, estate plans harness the trust creator's intent to ensure the family's financial capital enhances the lives of each family member, the family as a whole, and the communities and world in which they live.

But a plan is only as good as its execution. That's why, in the next chapter, the focus is on trust administration—how economic wealth is actually managed and experienced across generations.

Keys to Drafting Your Qualitative Estate Plan

- **Make it personal.** Give the trust a meaningful name. Draft it in the first person and use family names rather than referring to individuals as "beneficiaries" or a class of descendants. Ensure your descendants recognize your voice in your estate plan.

- **Declare your intention.** A simple declaration—"This trust is a gift of love intended to enhance the lives of the beneficiaries"—establishes clear intent. It signals that the trustee should focus on how the trust can support the flourishing of beneficiary family members and the family as a whole. If you want to go further, ensure the trustee is explicitly authorized to invest in family flourishing and provide guidance to the trustee with side letters to your trustee and descendants.

- **Build in flexibility.** Balance the technical rigor your lawyer rightly insists is required with the ability to adapt to sensible shifts and unforeseen changes in your family.

- **Leave a light on for the wayward.** Provide a path to redemption. Avoid absolutes and negative, punitive, or irreversible language. Leave an opening for people to grow and relationships to heal.

- **Set out a share for the family.** For example, if you have four children, consider creating a fifth share—for the family. Creating a family share establishes a pool of resources dedicated to the well-being of the family.

Keys to Drafting Your Qualitative Estate Plan (cont.)

- **Provide as much autonomy as possible.** Use separate trusts for individual members rather than shared or "pot" trusts. If possible, name beneficiaries as their own trustees, or possibly co-trustees. Or allow them to appoint and remove their trustees with reasonable guidelines.
- **Consider more lifetime gifts.** With increasing lifespans and growing economic capital, consider giving some financial wealth to your descendants *now* when it can make a meaningful difference, rather than on death. These gifts can be in a trust or outright gifts.
- **Avoid incentive trusts.** An incentive trust is designed to encourage specific behaviors or accomplishments by its beneficiaries and sets conditions that they must meet to qualify for distributions. Research has shown that money is typically an ineffective motivator of the very type of complex skills incentive trusts seek to motivate, like work ethic and responsible money management.
- **Establish a beneficiary relations committee.** This group will focus on ensuring the trust enhances the lives of each beneficiary and creates intentional focus on growing your family's human capital. The role of this group is much bigger than distributions; they will engage deeply with beneficiaries and help them learn to be accounted to by the trustee, which requires a clear understanding of their own role in relation to the trustee.

Have You Considered…
(For those who have created or are creating trusts)

- ❍ If you were to tear off the first and last page of your estate plan, would anyone reading it recognize *you* in it? What's missing?

- ❍ What name might you give your trust to capture what you truly hope it will do for your family?

- ❍ Imagine your grandchildren reading your estate plan 50 years from now. What do you want them to feel? What would you be embarrassed for them to find?

- ❍ Where in your estate planning might fear be doing the drafting—and where might love and possibility take its place?

- ❍ If you were a beneficiary of your own estate plan, would you experience it as a gift? What would you change if the answer is no?

For Families Already Living with Trusts

- ❍ Is the trust you live with today shaping your sense of agency and belonging? Does its administration feel like care, or just compliance?

From Insight to Action: What is your key takeaway?

Chapter Three

Qualitative Trust Administration

From Intent to Lived Experience

Authors' Note: *This chapter is addressed primarily to family members who are living as beneficiaries of trust structures created by others, and to the trustees and advisors who serve those beneficiaries.*

It also provides guidance to those individuals crafting or revising their estate plans, shedding light on what a positive experience can look like for the beneficiary-trustee relationship.

A WELL-DRAFTED ESTATE PLAN expresses intention. How the trusts created by that estate plan are administered determines whether that intention is ever felt in the lived experience of family members.

Trusts routinely outlive their creators and often outlive several generations of beneficiaries. While the drafting of a trust is a finite act, usually completed over a matter of months, trust administration is a lived process that unfolds over decades, impacting family members for generations.

It is during administration, not drafting, that descendants encounter their beneficial interest in property held in trust and experience whether it supports or undermines their overall well-being. This chapter is about that encounter: the moment when legal structure meets human reality.

Even the most thoughtfully designed trust can fail the people it was meant to serve if it is administered narrowly, mechanically, or defensively. On the other hand, a trust with imperfections can still become a genuine gift when it is administered with care, curiosity, and a deep sense of responsibility for the human beings involved.

A trust with imperfections can still become a genuine gift when it is administered with care, curiosity, and a deep sense of responsibility for the human beings involved.

Administration is where the gap between what was intended and what is experienced either widens or closes.

Like a constitution, a trust is not self-executing. Its words matter deeply, but words alone do not determine outcomes. Outcomes are shaped by interpretation, discretion, and the character of those entrusted with fiduciary authority.[26] The same document can enhance lives or undermine them depending on how it is brought to life. Drafting establishes the framework; administration gives it life.

The longer a trust is expected to last, the greater its potential for unintended consequences. Trust creators and their advisors are mortal; the trusts they create may endure for generations—and, in the case of perpetual or "dynasty" trusts, may be legally immortal. Some trusts are drafted decades before they ever "spring to life." As we've mentioned already, no one can foresee the lives, values, challenges, or environments of beneficiaries several generations removed, nor predict how dramatically circumstances may shift even between drafting and implementation.

The rise of perpetual trusts invites particular care. While the desire to protect assets across generations is understandable, perpetuity carries its own risks. History and lived experience suggest that long-lived wealth structures can unintentionally foster dependency, disengagement, or entitlement if human development is not intentionally cultivated alongside financial preservation. The question is not simply whether a trust can last forever, but whether it will remain life-enhancing across time. Administration therefore carries a responsibility not only to honor past intent but to remain attentive to present human lives as they unfold—and to design structures that reintroduce time, accountability, and growth into even the longest-lived arrangements. *This reality should invite humility.*

Maddie, Revisited: When a Trust Becomes a Lived Experience

After what she came to call "The Great Reveal," Maddie tried to do what she believed responsible adults were supposed to do. She continued to ask questions.

During one of her first annual meetings to review the trust, Maddie sat at the far end of the polished conference table that was beginning to feel familiar in a room that was clearly designed for board meetings rather than conversation. She followed along in the binder that had been placed in front of her as the trustee and counsel turned pages with practiced ease, moving from investment performance to distributions to tax reporting.

Overwhelmed and searching for some foothold, Maddie interrupted with a question that had been building in her for months. "How will I know if this trust is actually helping me live a good life?"

No one answered the question directly. There was an awkward pause, long enough for her to think someone might try. Then the meeting fell back into a predictable cadence with the trustee picking up at the next agenda item.

From a technical standpoint, everything appeared to be in order. Her trust statements arrived on time. The numbers reconciled. Requests were processed. Nothing was visibly broken. Yet Maddie experienced the trust not as a source of support but as a closed system: one she was expected to accept but not understand and to benefit from but not help shape.

The trust was being administered to her, not with her. Maddie was a beneficiary in name but not a person in relationship.

Over time, she stopped asking questions. Withdrawing became a way of preserving dignity. Maddie did not lose interest in living well; she simply came to feel that this trust was not a place where her questions—or she herself—belonged.

Trusts as Human Relationships

Every trust rests on a simple but often overlooked truth: A trust is a human relationship before it is a legal structure.

The law defines the relational framework in terms of roles, powers, and obligations, but it is the quality of the beneficiary/trustee relationship that determines how that framework is lived. No document, no matter how carefully drafted, can specify how power will be exercised, how discretion will feel to a beneficiary, or whether the trust will be experienced as a gift of love or a burden.

The ultimate question is not only whether the trustee complied with the law but whether the trust, as administered, fulfilled its highest purpose: Did it enhance the beneficiary's life?

Traditional trust administration often emphasizes compliance, documentation, and liability management, which are important concerns that shape how trustees approach their role. These things matter. They are essential. But they are not enough.

If the highest purpose of any trust is to enhance the life of the beneficiary—to support overall well-being, not merely to preserve or transfer economic capital—then accountability must be understood in deeper terms. The ultimate question is not only whether the trustee complied with the law but whether the trust, as administered, fulfilled its highest purpose: Did it enhance the beneficiary's life?

This question shifts accountability from compliance to impact. Intent matters, but intention that never becomes lived experience remains incomplete. Successful trust administration, therefore, demands attention not only to what the trust says but to what it does—to the ways it shapes agency, responsibility, confidence, and well-being over time.

If trusts are lived as human relationships rather than abstractions, then accountability must be understood in relational terms as well.

Accounting to the Beneficiary

The traditional perspective on "accounting to the beneficiary" means simply providing the beneficiary with sufficient financial reporting to satisfy baseline legal requirements.

While the law enshrines the trustee's duty to account, surely that duty involves more than reports delivered, decisions documented, assets prudently invested, distributions timely made, and procedures followed. These forms of accountability are necessary, but they do not address the deeper human question at the heart of the trust relationship.

Our view of "accounting to the beneficiary" is more expansive. We believe a trustee's duty includes being accountable for enhancing the well-being of each beneficiary, and it requires each beneficiary to be capable of evaluating whether their trustee is achieving this objective.[27] The duty of the trustee to account to the beneficiary with regard to the trust's life enhancement is not an ancillary feature of a trust; it is central to its existence.

A trust is not a gift. Ownership does not pass to the beneficiary. A trust exists because property has been entrusted to a trustee to hold for the benefit of another human being. A trustee has an inherent responsibility to prudently manage that property and to account to the beneficiary. Without a trustee's accounting, there is no way for the beneficiary to know whether the trustee is fulfilling that responsibility. Without accounting, there is no trust at all.

Without accounting, there is no trust at all.

Many trust relationships fail because these basics are neglected. But financial oversight and reporting alone cannot answer the deeper question of whether the trust is serving to enhance the life of the beneficiary.

A trust can be administered flawlessly on paper and still fail the human beings it was meant to serve. Trustees who rely exclusively on process without personal engagement risk mistaking compliance for care. While the law quite properly evaluates a trustee's process, families experience the outcomes.

True accountability requires a trustee who understands that their role is to serve a human life and a beneficiary who is capable of being accounted to. To account for a beneficiary's well-being requires humility. Trustees cannot fully know what constitutes a good life for another human being, nor can they assume competence in every domain of that life. Proceeding carefully—with a posture akin to "first, do no harm"—is itself part of a trustee's duty of care.

In our experience, almost no beneficiaries are taught how to evaluate whether a trust has enhanced their well-being, and almost no trustees are trained to understand that this is what accountability ultimately demands. As a result, both parties often misunderstand their roles. Trustees retreat into defensiveness, focused on risk and liability. Beneficiaries may withdraw into passivity, resentment, or entitlement. The relationship becomes static.

The qualitative trust administration we describe seeks to change this dynamic.[28]

The Role of the Trustee: Beyond Compliance

A great trustee is more than a capable technician. Technical competence is assumed. What distinguishes an exceptional trustee is not simply what they know but how they relate.

The trustee's role is not to parent beneficiaries, nor to control their choices or impose values. But neither is it to remain distant and procedural. The trustee we envision serves as a long-term steward and mentor—someone who helps create the conditions under which beneficiaries can grow into capable, responsible adults and integrate economic capital into lives of purpose and meaning.

At its best, trusteeship often looks like leadership from

behind. The trustee does not command the journey or dictate outcomes but instead shapes conditions. They ask thoughtful questions, offer perspective, and support growth without commandeering agency. This posture requires restraint as much as expertise, and humility as much as authority.

Because trusts last longer than people live, the most important decisions are rarely about whom to name as trustee. They are about defining attributes and processes. Trustees will come and go; what must endure is clarity about the qualities required to serve well and a process for selection, evaluation, and succession.

The Qualitative Trustee

The selection of trustees may be among the most consequential decisions in any long-term trust arrangement. Because trusts often endure for decades, and sometimes generations, this is rarely a single choice. Over time, multiple trustees will likely serve the family, and each transition presents a renewed opportunity to align administration with the family's commitment to flourishing.

As we've already said, technical expertise and analytical ability are essential. A trustee must understand fiduciary law, tax implications, investment principles, and governance mechanics. These are not optional. They are baseline competencies. But a qualitative trustee requires more than competence. The long arc of trust administration also demands character and relational capacity.

Personal Attributes of a Qualitative Trustee

A trustee who supports flourishing is doing their own developmental work and often demonstrates:

- **Emotional intelligence.** The ability to listen without defensiveness, recognize unspoken dynamics, and respond with empathy rather than authority alone. Discretion is exercised not only through analysis but also understanding.
- **Spiritual intelligence.** Not in a religious sense, but as an awareness of meaning, values, and purpose. A qualitative trustee understands that financial capital exists in service to human well-being and can engage respectfully in conversations about purpose and aspiration.
- **Poise and presence.** The capacity to remain steady amid tension, conflict, or strong emotion. Trust administration often unfolds during vulnerable moments. A trustee's calm becomes a stabilizing force.
- **Patience.** Development takes time. Families mature across decades. A qualitative trustee resists urgency when growth requires space.
- **Humility and curiosity.** A willingness to ask questions, learn, and avoid the assumption that technical knowledge confers relational wisdom. The best trustees continue to grow alongside the families they serve.
- **A growth mindset.** The belief that beneficiaries are capable of development. Rather than viewing individuals as fixed risks to be managed, the trustee sees potential to be supported.
- **Gratitude and perspective.** An appreciation for the privilege of serving in a fiduciary role. Trustees who see their work as stewardship rather than control tend to foster healthier, more resilient relationships.

Personal Attributes of a Qualitative Trustee (cont.)

Warning signs

Just as important as identifying positive qualities is recognizing warning signs that the trustee is not a good fit. Families should be cautious of trustees who rely exclusively on technical authority, dismiss beneficiary concerns as immaturity or entitlement, or default to rigid adherence to policy when discretion calls for judgment. A trustee who is chronically unavailable, defensive when questioned, or uncomfortable discussing purpose and values may struggle to administer a long-term trust in a qualitative way. Similarly, an excessive focus on control, risk avoidance, or liability protection at the expense of relational engagement can erode trust between fiduciary and beneficiary.

Over time, these patterns may produce compliance but not confidence and structure but not stewardship. In the end, the character of the trustee will shape the lived experience of the trust as much as its legal provisions.

The Qualitative Trustee in Action

Consider how one family trustee chose to inhabit this role.

Evan is a third-generation member of a family with long-standing trusts. When his cousin Marco asked him to serve as trustee for Marco's children, Leo and Sofía, Evan agreed, expecting a tidy, mainly functionary role. What he did not expect was how the work would shape him. The first request came quickly. Leo called about a summer robotics program.

"What will you learn?" Evan asked.

"Not just coding," Leo said. "Teamwork. Failing fast. Trying again."

"Good," Evan replied. "Afterward, tell me what changed because you went."

Leo's recap was not a list of activities, but a story of resilience and collaboration. Evan began to see that he was not simply approving distributions. He was helping shape decisions that grow people.

Over time, Evan refined a process for administering the trust. Each request prompted three questions: What will you learn? Who will guide you? What will you give back? Approvals became votes for a young person's future. "Not yet" became an invitation to return with clearer purpose.

"People think trustees are gatekeepers. We're gardeners. We help the seeds take root."

Years later, when his own daughter, Maya, was preparing to approach her trustee for a distribution so she could apply for a community health fellowship, Evan suggested the same framework.

"Go to your trustee with answers to these three questions," Evan said. "What will you learn? Who will mentor you? What's the give-back?"

The framework transformed requests into plans, and plans into progress. Rather than imposing restrictions, it probed readiness.

Not every one of Evan's answers was yes. One nephew beneficiary returned with a distribution request that felt more like convenience than calling. Evan replied, "Not yet." He offered guidance and left the door open. Months later, the proposal returned. This time the nephew had identified a mentor, a timeline, and a clearer purpose.

At a holiday gathering, the cousins began sharing their "finest requests." The robotics program became a scholarship essay. An internship led to employment. The fellowship evolved into research. The apprenticeship culminated in an exhibit for younger cousins. The approval became secondary to the growth.

Evan later reflected, "I thought trustee work was document management. It turns out it's a way to grow the future."

When he stepped back from the trustee role, he left behind learning plans, mentor check-ins, teach-backs—and a simple family motto: "Receive with purpose. Steward with care." While it took a bit more time, the teach-backs proved to be an important practice to confirm the information provided was being understood by getting people to "teach back" what had been discussed.

Welcoming the next trustee, he added one final thought: "People think trustees are gatekeepers. We're gardeners. We help the seeds take root."

Trustee as Mentor, Not Parent

Beneficiaries change over time. A child, adolescent, young adult, and mature adult each require very different forms of engagement. Qualitative administration recognizes these differences and adapts accordingly.

Beneficiaries do not develop all at once; their needs, capacities, and questions change across stages of life. Administration that focuses on the success of this beneficiary at a particular moment in time becomes adaptive rather than rigid and supportive rather than controlling. This intentional focus on the role of time at play in a beneficiary's phase of life is one of the most powerful antidotes to entropic drift.

As beneficiaries mature, the trustee's posture should evolve:

With children	becoming a familiar and trustworthy presence, invited into relationship with the child by the parents.
With adolescents	introducing conversations about responsibility and the meaning of true well-being and the supporting role of economic capital; supporting the parents' journey of raising healthy, responsible children.
With young adults	engaging as a mentor; asking what is going well, what is challenging, and how the trust might support growth rather than replace effort.
With adults	engaging as peers, deepening the relationship and bringing life enhancement to reality.
With elders	supporting the evolution to valued, generative leader.

Trustees should not act in the place of parents. Parents remain parents. But trustees can support families by reinforcing growth, accountability, and learning—without undermining parental authority.

Importantly, when the relationship with the beneficiary is strong, trustees rarely need to say "no." Requests tend to align naturally with the trust's purpose because understanding is shared.

Qualitative trustees remember to factor in the role of time in the trust relationship. Maturation matters. Adult beneficiaries, given appropriate information and opportunity, are treated as adults, with voice, dignity, and participation. This expectation does not relieve trustees of duty; it provides a developmental horizon against which administration can be measured.

The Moral Gap—and the Role of the Beneficiary

Trusts create an inherent moral gap. The trustee holds legal authority and responsibility over property while the beneficiary enjoys benefits of that property as a matter of right. This separation of rights from responsibility has the potential to undermine beneficiary development by removing the natural feedback loops through which people usually learn. The law imposes no duties on beneficiaries, assigning a passive role with regard to responsibility for the assets, but human flourishing thrives when responsibility is connected to the benefits of ownership.

Over time, trust systems that do not intentionally

cultivate responsibility and personal agency tend toward a kind of entropy. The human energy that once created the wealth—creativity, work, and purpose—can gradually dissipate into dependence, disengagement, and malaise. When economic capital becomes disconnected from responsibility, beneficiaries may lose not only motivation but a sense of authorship over their own lives. Administration that ignores this drift risks preserving assets at the expense of human well-being.

Some parents, for example, are concerned that a child may not learn to save or might spend too much as a beneficiary. One way to handle this would be through incentive trust provisions that try to control from the grave, such as a term that trust distributions could only be made to "match" an heir's personal savings. These restrictive provisions, however, can backfire, either by creating resentment or by being ill-suited to the circumstances of a beneficiary's life as it evolves over time. Another way to handle this is through the trustee and beneficiary relationship. A trustee empowered as a true mentor will help the beneficiary learn financial responsibility, rather than enforce an arcane and ill-fitting trust provision.

Trust systems that do not intentionally cultivate responsibility and personal agency tend toward a kind of entropy.

For a trust to enhance well-being, beneficiaries must grow into maturity not because the document demands it, but because the relationship invites it and is in the best interest of the beneficiary. A mature beneficiary takes responsibility for understanding the trust and can articulate what enhancement means in their own life. They engage in meaningful work or contribution, reflect on dependency and agency, and enjoy the benefits of economic capital without guilt or entitlement.

These responsibilities cannot be enforced. They must be cultivated. And that takes time.

Structures That Support Qualitative Administration

Governance structures matter—but only when they serve relationships rather than replace them.

A simple trust, well administered, outperforms a complex structure that lacks purpose. Trust committees, trust protectors, directed trustees, and private trust companies can support family well-being when they are designed to elevate accountability, continuity, and care. But complexity should never be adopted for its own sake.

Where more robust governance is appropriate, clarity is essential. Decision-making authority must be understood. Beneficiaries should have appropriate access and voice. Boards and committees should regularly remind themselves that their ultimate responsibility is not to a pool of economic capital but to a group of human beings.

Here is a useful standing question for any governing body to consider: Is there anything we could be doing to enhance the well-being of the beneficiaries that we are not yet doing?

Trustee Transition and Succession

Because many trusts endure for decades, trustee service will almost always involve transition. Retirement, resignation, incapacity, institutional change, or shifting family needs make succession inevitable. For this reason, trustee selection is not a single event but an ongoing governance responsibility.

A qualitative approach to trustee transition treats succession as a moment of reflection rather than disruption. Families can ask:

- Does the current structure still reflect our values and needs?
- What qualities are most needed in this season of the trust's life?
- Has the family's complexity changed in ways that require different capacities?

Trustee succession should not be driven solely by convenience or habit. Nor should it be reactive, triggered only by crisis. Instead, thoughtful plans often include:

- clear succession provisions in the trust instrument;
- defined mechanisms for appointment and removal;
- periodic review of trustee performance; and
- opportunities for emerging generations to understand how trustees are selected and evaluated.

Transition also provides a chance to recalibrate expectations. Each new trustee inherits not only legal authority but also relational dynamics. Intentional communication during transition can preserve trust, clarify roles, and reinforce shared purpose.

As with all aspects of qualitative administration, the goal is not simply continuity of management but continuity of care.

Not Too Late

Beneficiaries are often born into trust structures they did not design. They may experience these trusts as rigid, impersonal, or opaque. Similarly, trustees are often appointed by trust documents that offer little guidance to them beyond technical rules focused on financial capital.

It is not too late.

Even when a trust lacks explicit language of intent, trustees and beneficiaries can work together to articulate purpose. Precatory statements, shared understanding, and a changed posture can transform administration without changing a single word of the trust document. Trust documents set the stage, but they do not dictate the quality of the performance. It remains in the hands of the trustee and beneficiary to choose how their roles are inhabited.

As we have said previously, at its highest level, a trust is meant to function as a gift of love. Even where that language is not explicit in the trust document, trustees and beneficiaries can choose to adopt this posture together. Naming purpose, openly and repeatedly, can restore orientation and meaning to trusts that have become rigid, impersonal, or purely procedural.

Trusts do not help families flourish because the documents are perfectly drafted. Families flourish when members are willing to grow.

A Note on Private Trust Companies

Some families consider establishing a private trust company (PTC) as their trust structures grow in size or complexity. When thoughtfully designed, a PTC can offer continuity, alignment, and deeper engagement with a family's long-term aspirations. When approached primarily as a technical upgrade, however, it can simply reproduce existing challenges at greater scale.

A family should consider a PTC only if it is prepared to do more than alternative arrangements require, not less. Unlike external trusteeship, a PTC places the family closer to the center of responsibility. It magnifies the family's culture, values, and habits, for better or worse.

Importantly, a well-run PTC is a significant undertaking. It requires sustained investment in infrastructure, governance systems, compliance oversight, and—perhaps most critically—talent. Qualified directors, experienced fiduciary professionals, administrative support, and thoughtful coordination with advisors are not optional features; they are foundational. Without this level of commitment, a PTC risks becoming either symbolic or overburdened.

When effective, a PTC goes well beyond managing assets. It becomes a platform for learning, stewardship, and relationship, supporting the development of human, intellectual, social, and spiritual capital alongside financial capital. In this sense, a PTC is less an administrative solution and more an expression of how a family chooses to live with its wealth.

PTCs also offer the possibility of designing a board of directors who bring deep qualitative expertise, including the ability to engage beneficiaries and foster development. They also offer flexibility to create beneficiary relations committees focused directly on this work.

Clarity of roles is essential. A PTC must be thoughtfully positioned in relation to operating company boards and other governance structures, respecting appropriate boundaries while enabling coordination. When roles blur, even well-intentioned structures can undermine trust and agency.

A Note on Private Trust Companies (cont.)

For some families, a PTC becomes a powerful vehicle for flourishing. For others, different arrangements better serve the same ends. The question is not which structure is most sophisticated, but which best reflects the family's readiness to invest time, attention, and resources in stewarding both relationships and responsibilities over the long term.[29]

A Bridge Forward

Qualitative trust administration cannot replace family culture—but it can reinforce it, protect it, and even prevent harm.

Trust administration shapes daily experience. Family culture shapes meaning. Investing in relationship, learning, personal development and care, while embracing technical excellence, makes a difference.

Families who choose this different posture often experience deeper connection, greater resilience, and a shared sense of purpose over time. In these families, the trust plays a supporting role—becoming a long-lived part of the family system and a stabilizing presence that helps sustain well-being and flourishing.

In the next chapter, we turn from the trust system itself to the family system it serves—exploring how families cultivate the habits, practices, and shared purpose that allow well-being to endure across generations.

Have You Considered …
(For Families Already Living with Trusts)

- Think of a time you felt genuinely *seen* by someone in an institutional role—a teacher, a mentor, a doctor. What made the difference? Does your trust relationship feel anything like that?

- What would change in your family's trust relationship if the central question shifted from *Were the rules followed?* to *Were lives enhanced?*

- If you are a beneficiary: If your trustee were to ask you, "How will I know if this trust is enhancing your life?" what would you say? Have you ever been asked?

- What does a "qualitative trustee" look like to you? Do you have one? Are you one?

- If you are serving as a trustee: Are you a gatekeeper or a gardener? What would it look like to tend rather than guard?

- What's one thing you could do—right now, without changing a single legal document—to make the trust feel more like a relationship and less like an imposed arrangement?

From Insight to Action: What is your key takeaway?

Chapter Four

Qualitative Family Culture
A Culture of Care Where Flourishing Takes Root

A FAMILY DOES NOT FLOURISH because it has a well-designed estate plan. An estate plan exists to serve a family, not to create one.

This distinction is easy to miss, particularly in families with significant financial wealth. Legal and financial structures are visible, measurable, and familiar. Over time, families may come to believe, often unconsciously, that the right documents, trustees, and controls will secure the future. They will not.

At its deepest level, culture reflects a family's orientation toward life itself. What do we aspire to become? What do we believe is larger than any one of us? What do we care about enough to sustain attention over time? These questions and others shape how families understand success, responsibility, and belonging. This shared orientation is what we mean by spiritual capital. It is not doctrine or belief, but the aspiration and practice that gives coherence and meaning to family life across generations.

Estate plans and trusts can preserve resources and shape experience, but they cannot generate meaning, character, belonging, and connection. Those emerge only from a culture of care. This chapter is about that deeper work. The work that, over many years, creates the family's true lived experience and legacy. This is what a qualitative estate plan is crafted to protect, and what qualitative trust administration is intended to sustain.

Spiritual capital is not doctrine or belief, but the aspiration and practice that gives coherence and meaning to family life across generations.

Culture Is the True Source of Family Legacy

Every family has a culture, whether it is named or not. Culture is not only what a family says it values, but also, "the way things are done around here." It is how family members behave when confronted with difficult decisions; it is how they behave when no one is watching.

A family's culture also shapes how conflict is handled, how difference is tolerated, how success is defined, and how failure is treated. When financial capital enters the picture, family culture does not disappear. It is amplified.

This is why estate plans and trusts never operate in isolation. They exist in the cultural context of the family that creates them.

As Matthew Wesley has observed in his work in multigenerational families,[30] culture does more than

A welcoming family grounded in openness, good communication, learning, and accountability will often be capable of using imperfect structures well.

A family shaped by secrecy, fear, or control will struggle even with thoughtful and well-crafted planning documents.

influence whether structures succeed. Structures only work when they align with the family's culture. No matter how carefully designed, structures that run against the grain of family culture tend to be ignored, undermined, or repurposed. In this sense, culture can supplant structure entirely. This is why getting family culture right is the highest priority for a family.

A flourishing family is not built around an estate plan—a structure. But an estate plan can be built to support a flourishing family. For example, we have seen a family whose estate plan was well drafted but experienced as distant and opaque by the rising generation. Conversations with the trustee were limited to annual reviews, and engagement was low. By coming together as beneficiaries to name their purpose more explicitly and enhance how the trust was administered, including regular opportunities to touch base with the trustee, developing opportunities for shared learning on topics of their choice, and setting out clearer expectations for the trustee's role, the family began to experience the plan not as a structure imposed upon them but as a support for their growth. Over time, relationships deepened and participation increased.

The Courage to Welcome

Every family that hopes to endure must eventually face a quiet and uncomfortable truth: No family survives on blood alone.

Families begin when two strangers choose one another. Whatever fragments of shared DNA may follow, what truly binds a family together are bonds of affinity—chosen commitments, renewed over time. A family's future depends not on preserving "our blood," but on welcoming new members who were once, and in some sense always remain, strangers.

Each generation must choose to join. And welcome.

Marriage is not absorption. It is not conquest. It is not entry into a preexisting fortress. It is an act of courage—a leap of hope toward people whose history, habits, anxieties, and imperfections one is voluntarily choosing to inherit. When someone joins a family by marriage or partnership, they are not only being selected. They are doing the selecting.

They are choosing your **stories**.

Your **unresolved conflicts**.

Your **traditions**.

Your **vulnerabilities**.

Your **culture**.

Every generation after them must choose again, not only choosing each other but choosing those who arrive at the threshold: spouses, partners, and in-laws who—in addition to choosing you—trust you with their stories, strengths, and vulnerabilities.

Belonging is not a possession to guard; it is a gift that must be offered, received, and renewed. This is the structure by which families continue—how traditions stay alive, how character is refined, and how every form of wealth grows when shared.

The question before us all is simple and searching: Will we be a fortress that protects what we have, or a table that makes room for all those who come?

Moving from Fear to Courage

It is easy, particularly in families with significant financial wealth, to slip into protective instincts. Fear can distort perception. New members may be viewed through the lens of risk: outsider, disrupter, fortune seeker, threat. These narratives, often unspoken, erode the very foundations they claim to defend.

A family that seeks flourishing must confront this fear honestly.

If a family forgets that it began with an act of hope between strangers, it may drift toward suspicion instead of hospitality. Over time, that posture becomes self-defeating. The future of the family depends entirely on the willingness of each rising generation to form what might be called a horizontal compact—an affirmative decision to join one another in shared responsibility and shared becoming.

This is not sentimentality. It is structural reality.

- Without welcoming, continuity becomes fragile.
- Without courage, renewal becomes difficult.
- Without choice, belonging slowly fades.

Inviting Belonging

As Brené Brown elegantly states: "Belonging is the innate human desire to be part of something larger than us."[31]

To invite belonging, to genuinely welcome, is not to abandon discernment or boundaries. It is to recognize that flourishing requires openness—that love must be extended, not guarded like property. Welcoming is an act of humility. It acknowledges that no family owns its future. The future is given by those who choose to enter it.

At its heart, a welcoming family understands something simple and profound: Belonging is not inherited automatically. It is offered, received, and renewed. By welcoming, the family expands their world and seeds durability for a connected future.

Open Mind, Heart, and Will

Channeling Otto Scharmer's Theory U[32] can strengthen the welcoming of a new family member by applying Scharmer's three essential "openings":

- An **open mind (curiosity)** that suspends judgment and approaches the newcomer with genuine curiosity rather than preconceived notions.

- An **open heart (compassion)** that feels authentic compassion for the person's experience of transition and change.

- An **open will (courage)** that acknowledges how this person's presence will reshape family identity itself, rather than treating integration as a logistical process of fitting someone into existing family patterns.

Scharmer's framework invites families to practice what he calls "presencing"—a simultaneous awareness that honors both who the family has been and who they might become. When families welcome newcomers through this three-dimensional openness, they open the door to create genuine belonging grounded not in surface politeness but in authentic connection and mutual transformation.

The most important sentence a family can say, and mean, may be this: "We each welcome you to our family with an open heart, mind, and will, and with deep appreciation for your choosing us."

If this sentence is true, the family's future is alive.

The most important sentence a family can say, and mean, may be this: "We each welcome you to our family with an open heart, mind, and will, and with deep appreciation for your choosing us."

From Financial Focus to Family Flourishing

Families often devote enormous energy, time, and expense to stewarding their financial capital. This is understandable. Money is tangible, measurable, and vulnerable to loss. But as we have covered previously, economic capital is only one form of wealth, and it is not the most important one.

The capacity of family members to live meaningful, responsible lives of connection and service plays a significant role in determining whether the financial capital serves as a gift or a burden. It is family resilience, curiosity, self-knowledge, purpose, and skills that matter more over time than any monetary asset on its balance sheet.

> ***When financial capital is held in service to human, intellectual, social, and spiritual development, it becomes a means of enabling possibility rather than an end in itself.***

Families that flourish invest intentionally in people.[33] Preparing the rising generation is not primarily about teaching them how to manage money. It is about helping them understand who they are, what they value, and how they contribute.

Over time, many families discover that financial capital has a purpose beyond its own growth. Its deepest role is not accumulation, but support. When financial capital is held in service to human, intellectual, social, and spiritual development, it becomes a means of enabling possibility rather than an end in itself. Without that orientation, even abundance can feel hollow or destabilizing.

Growing family members is not an expense. It is the central work of a family and requires being fully present with an open mind (suspend judgment), open heart (cultivate empathic connection) and open will (let go and let come).[34]

The Integration Problem Revisited

Earlier, we described inheritance as a meteor, something that can arrive suddenly and with enormous force. Whether that impact destabilizes a life or can be absorbed over time depends in large part on family culture. A healthy family culture prepares the next generation for the arrival of financial wealth—the meteor.

Learning to live with money is not a legal process; it is a human one. It takes time, conversation, and context. It also requires an environment in which questions are welcome, mistakes are not fatal, and identity is not defined by entitlement or restriction.

When families lack this culture of trust, they often respond to challenges by tightening control. Rules multiply. Conditions harden. Discretion shrinks. These responses may feel protective, but they often increase fragility rather than reduce it.

Wesley[35] describes this reflex as a structuralist impulse, the belief that better rules, tighter controls, or more elaborate systems can resolve fundamentally human challenges. In families, this often leads to an accumulation of structures intended to manage risk but instead inadvertently increase distance, rigidity, or disengagement. When this happens, the problem is not a failure of design, but a misreading of what the family system actually needs.

Strong culture allows families to hold complexity without panic. It creates space for learning, difference, and growth over time.

Maddie's Awakening

The shift did not begin with a document. It began with a question from one of her children.

After a family gathering, riding home in the dark, her eldest asked from the back seat, "Why does everyone get so strange when money comes up?" Maddie looked out the window and did not answer right away. She knew exactly what her daughter meant: the elephant in the room. The quick change of subject. The half-finished explanations. The sense that something important was present, but not available for honest conversation.

That question stayed with her. She began to see that what unsettled her most about her own inheritance was not the money itself, but the absence of any context and guidance that could help her make sense of it. There had been no shared language, no gradual preparation, and no place to ask what it all meant for her life. The trustee had appeared suddenly, and the structure arrived fully formed. The human context for her to make meaning of it had not.

That realization brought relief. For the first time, the challenge felt less ambiguous and more understandable, and therefore manageable. Maddie and Omar began talking more deliberately about the kind of family they wanted to be. They were not ready with a comprehensive plan. In fact, they fumbled their way through several of their early discussions with the kids. But they were ready with a refusal: Silence would not do the shaping in their home. They began to speak earlier and more plainly with their children about hard work, contribution, money, and how they viewed their resources as an opportunity that came with responsibility—rather than an entitlement. They shared their own worries and discussed each other's expectations.

Maddie also began to engage differently with the trustee. She no longer looked to the trust to provide meaning it could not provide. Instead, she approached the relationship as one human being dealing with another inside an imperfect structure. The legal arrangement had not changed. Her stance had. For the first time, she felt less trapped inside a system she had not chosen and more capable of deciding how she would live within it.

Learning as Adaptation

Flourishing families share a critical capability: the ability to learn.

Learning, at its core, is self-initiated change. It is how human beings adapt when circumstances shift and assumptions no longer hold. A big part of adult learning involves unlearning.[36] In a world of constant social, economic, and technological change, families that cannot learn are forced to rely on control. Families that can learn remain flexible.

One reason culture so often overwhelms structure is that culture is lived before it is understood. Families experience culture not as policy or principle, but as patterns, roles, and unspoken rules that shape behavior over time. Learning, therefore, cannot be imposed through structure alone. It emerges when families become curious about their own patterns and open to experiencing themselves differently.

This kind of learning requires more than problem-solving. It involves a shift in awareness. Families move from asking, "What do we want and how will we get it?" to the deeper question, "What is life showing us now?" This posture of curiosity and reflection allows families to engage change without needing to dominate it. Learning, in this sense, is not about mastery, but about participation in an unfolding life.

A legacy is not something you leave; it is something you live.

Learning in families is not limited to formal education or financial literacy, and it is not the sole domain of the rising generation. It is for the entire family to adopt a lifelong learning mindset. It includes learning about relationships, responsibility, work, failure, and meaning. It requires reflection, dialogue, and the willingness to revise long-held beliefs.

Skills and knowledge that once lasted a lifetime now require continual renewal. In families that take culture seriously, learning becomes less about preparation for a distant future and more about how life is lived in the present. Curiosity is encouraged. Exploration is welcomed. Learning is understood as an ongoing pursuit rather than a finite phase.

Over time, this orientation toward learning shapes more than individual competence. It influences how families relate to change, how they collaborate across differences, and how they understand their role in the wider world. When learning is embedded in family culture, it becomes one of the ways families invest in holistic well-being, creating conditions for each generation to flourish.

A culture that values learning prepares family members to integrate change, including the arrival of financial capital, without losing coherence.

Habits of Flourishing Families

Flourishing families do not share identical values or structures, but they do tend to share certain habits. These are not rules to be enforced. They are patterns that emerge when families take human development seriously.[37]

- **They talk early and often.** Conversations about money, work, expectations, and responsibility begin before crises force them into the open. Information is shared over time, unfolding in age-appropriate ways, not withheld until disclosure becomes traumatic.

- **They normalize learning.** Curiosity is encouraged. Mistakes are treated as feedback, not failure. (We like to use as a mantra the acronym FAIL: "First Attempt In Learning.") Growth matters more than performance.

- **They value contribution over consumption.** Family members are expected to engage in work, service, or creative pursuits that give shape to their lives. Identity is not anchored in resources, but in participation, contribution, and purpose.

- **They make room for difference.** Flourishing families understand that sameness is not the goal. Different paths are tolerated and celebrated without revoking belonging.

- **They embrace feedback as a gift.** Leveraging the ideas of deliberately developmental organizations[38] in the family, they treat every day as practice ground for growth. They frame feedback as fuel rather than judgment. They share rituals—such as end-of-day check-ins, like, "One thing I'm working on ..." And they name their growth edges and share quick feed-forward requests.

Over time, these habits do more than shape individual lives. They create a sense of "we." Families become a community not through shared assets or shared rules, but through sustained care for one another across difference, disagreement, and change. This sense of connection, of belonging to something larger than oneself, is a central expression of spiritual capital. Without it, there may be coordination or coexistence, but there is no enduring sense of meaning or affinity.

These habits cannot be legislated. They must be nurtured and practiced.

The Capacity for Play

One of the most overlooked attributes of flourishing families is their capacity for play.

Play does not mean frivolity. It means curiosity instead of fear, experimentation instead of abiding by rigid structures, and growth instead of perfection. Play is how human beings learn. And play is not the exclusive domain of children. Almost all highly evolved animals spend a fair amount of time at play right through adulthood. Consider our own penchant for sports, dance, games, parties. Play is integral to our well-being.

Across cultures and generations, play has long been woven into family life—appearing in stories, rituals, celebrations, and shared gatherings. Long before families spoke explicitly about development or education, they intuitively understood that play helped transmit values and strengthen bonds while welcoming the next generation into the life of the group. When this spirit of play is brought into family gatherings, people stay engaged and connected, returning year after year. Families that lose the ability to play often become brittle. They mistake control for care and obedience for loyalty. Over time, this rigidity makes it difficult to absorb new generations, new ideas, or new realities without fracture.

Play is how human beings learn. And play is not the exclusive domain of children.

Families that retain the capacity for play can hold structure and freedom at the same time. They set boundaries, but they also invite participation. They allow family members to rehearse roles while making mistakes and growing into responsibility.

Families sometimes confuse freedom with the absence of care. In practice, the opposite is true. The ability to be carefree is an earned freedom that grows out of a sense of responsibility, fueled by purpose and anchored by belonging. Play flourishes in this kind of freedom, grounded rather than unmoored.

Additionally, when families are grounded in spiritual capital, they are better able to hold uncertainty without panic, because their sense of meaning is not dependent on control or certainty, but on care, connection, and shared aspiration.

Play creates agency. It allows family members to experience themselves not as performers following a script written by others, but as participants in a shared and evolving story.

A Culture of Care, Not Control

Fear is a powerful force in families with significant financial capital: fear of loss, misuse, regret, not living up to the revered accomplishments of past generations, and being blamed by future generations.

When fear dominates, control often follows. Rules multiply. Flexibility diminishes. Dialogue narrows. Anxiety increases.

A culture of care responds differently. Care does not eliminate boundaries, but it changes the posture with which boundaries are held. It replaces surveillance with dialogue and punishment with accountability. For example, one family had seen how a fear of misuse crystallized in a decades-old trust deed with detailed rules and restrictions around trust distributions. While intended to protect, these strict rules led to reduced dialogue and increased anxiety among beneficiaries. When this family intentionally shifted toward a posture of care and curiosity, engaging in open conversation, clarifying expectations, and working with the trustee to encourage a view toward using discretion to support growth, the dynamic changed. Boundaries remained, but they were experienced as supportive rather than controlling, leading to greater trust and responsibility over time.

Care is purposeful attention directed toward the flourishing of real human lives over time.

Care, as we use the term here, is not therapeutic nor sentimental. It is purposeful attention directed toward the flourishing of real human lives over time. Care, in this sense, is not merely behavioral. It reflects a deeper commitment to seeing one another as whole people, connected across time, and worthy of dignity regardless of outcome. This is one of the ways spiritual capital is lived, not proclaimed, in family life.

A culture of care becomes real only when care is specific. Families do not flourish by agreeing on abstract values alone, but by attending to particular people in particular seasons of life with curiosity and humility. What supports one family member at one moment may be constraining to another (or even to the same person at a different time).

Families oriented toward care understand that values cannot be enforced indefinitely from beyond the grave. They must be lived, modeled, and renewed in each generation.

A culture of care is tested most clearly when a family member becomes difficult.

Cultivating Care with Difficult Family Members

Every family that stays together long enough will have a difficult member. The instinct is often to manage around the person, contain them, or quietly resent them. Flourishing families take a different approach. They build a system of care strong enough to hold complexity and address these challenges. This requires a shift from reacting to behavior to designing an environment.

Most families wait to address their decision-making needs until conflict erupts, resulting in a system built under stress. A system of care is built in calmer seasons, before a rupture. It assumes that strong personalities, old wounds, mental health struggles, and power imbalances are not exceptions but part of the landscape.[39]

Rather than treating difficulty as an anomaly, flourishing families design for it. They build layered support: coaches, governance advisors, and sometimes family therapists. They invest in developing shared language, conflict resilience, and the capacity to examine their respective roles in their system. They open doors and windows for growth.

When fear dominates, families tighten control. When

care leads, they strengthen the system instead.

A system of care is not soft but sturdy. It allows disagreement and even recurring tension to exist without tearing the fabric of the family. Stability does not depend on one person behaving well. It depends on the strength of care and on the shared commitment to remain in relationship while continuing to grow. The goal is not to eliminate difficulty. It is to create a culture where growth, accountability, and compassion coexist.

> ***When fear dominates, families tighten control.***

Care is grounded in reality and sometimes requires hard choices. One family council struggled with a cousin who repeatedly derailed meetings with personal attacks and refused to follow agreed norms. Rather than escalating conflict or withdrawing in frustration, the council clarified a boundary: participation required behavior that protected the group's ability to function. They paused the cousin's attendance and laid out a clear path back to participating in family meetings, which included engaging with a coach and committing to upholding meeting protocols.

This approach reflects a deeper principle. As Dennis Jaffe's multigenerational research suggests, families that flourish operate on "free choice" to "remain partners."[40] Adult family members are not held in the system by guilt, pressure, or bloodline. They choose to remain engaged.

This principle becomes especially important when difficulty arises. Choice preserves dignity and reduces power struggles because no one is being held hostage. Responsibility rests where it belongs—with each individual, who must decide whether they are committed to fostering the family's culture of care. The goal of the family is one of attraction: to make the system compelling enough that each family member chooses to belong. A flourishing family is not one without difficult members. It is one that refuses to let difficulty define its culture.

Culture Creates Choice

Culture does not guarantee harmony or eliminate conflict. It creates choice.

Families with healthy culture are better able to respond thoughtfully rather than react defensively. They are more capable of revisiting their assumptions and adjusting course with greater clarity about what lies ahead. In the final chapter, we turn to that forward-looking work. Having explored why flourishing matters, how planning and administration can support it, and why culture is indispensable, we ask the final question: How then shall we live?

A Note for Families Already Living with Trusts

Many families are already living with trusts they did not design. These structures may feel rigid. Relationships may feel impersonal. Options for change may appear limited.

While there are legal avenues to explore to amend trust and estate documents, even when they cannot be rewritten, culture can be shaped. Posture can change. Conversations can begin. Trustees can engage differently. Beneficiaries can step into their roles with greater voice and agency. The script you inherited may not be one you would have written. But you still choose how to perform it.

Families cannot always change the structure they inherited, but they can influence the experience of living within it, and they can prepare the rising generation differently.

Have You Considered...

- What's one tradition, phrase, or habit in your family that quietly says, *This is who we are*—for better or worse?

- Think of someone who married into your family. How welcomed did they truly feel? How do you know?

- When your family hits a challenging time, does it tend toward *control* or *care*? What would it take to lean more toward care?

- What's a mistake someone in your family made that actually taught everyone something important? Was it treated that way at the time?

- Is there a "difficult" family member your system is designed *around* rather than *for*? What might it look like to design *for* them instead?

- If your family culture were a piece of music, what would it sound like right now—and what would you want it to sound like in 20 years?

From Insight to Action: What is your key takeaway?

Chapter Five

Becoming Authors of the Future

From Culture to Choice

EVERY FAMILY REACHES a moment when reflection must give way to choice.

We have invited you to reconsider what you mean when you use the word *wealth*—not as a synonym for money or assets, but as a fuller measure of human well-being lived over time, across relationships, and in community. This shift is not semantic. It reorients how you think about wealth. It asks you to look beyond accumulation and toward the conditions that allow people and families to flourish.

We have explored how estate planning and trust administration can either support or undermine that flourishing. We have argued that culture, more than structure, determines whether financial capital becomes a gift or a burden. None of this, however, decides what your family will do next.

Documents do not decide. Advisors do not decide. Even culture, as powerful as it is, does not decide.

People do.

The script may shape the performance, but it does not fix the ending.

This final chapter is about that moment of authorship—when a family decides how intentionally it wishes to live and what it is willing to invest in order to support that life across generations.

This chapter is not about adding complexity. It is about choosing direction.

Choosing to Act, Not Just to Understand

Insight alone does not change families.

Many families understand what matters long before they act on it. The difference between families who flourish and those who stagnate is rarely intelligence or access to advice. It is willingness.

- Willingness to speak and stay in conversation, even when uncomfortable.
- Willingness to decide without perfect certainty.
- Willingness to lead.
- Willingness to trust one another over time.
- Willingness to take risks and make difficult decisions.

Choosing to move forward is not an escape from responsibility; it is an embrace of it.

Intentional families understand that the work will always remain unfinished, outcomes will be imperfect, and learning will continue. Responsibility is not a burden imposed from outside. It is the natural companion to authorship.

For some families, action begins with small steps. Conversations start earlier. Information is shared more openly. Expectations around work and contribution become clearer. For others, the choice is more explicit. They bring in new advisors, take on new roles, and commit to ongoing learning and development.

There is no single correct path. There is only intentional movement.

Choosing to act also means choosing to engage differences and resolve disputes rather than avoid hard conversations. These are not evidence of failure but a natural consequence of shared history, shared resources, and shared futures. Families rarely fracture because of differences and disputes. They fracture when dialogue stops and systems freeze.[41]

Getting Unstuck

Leadership turns reflection into momentum.

In many families, inertia sets in quietly. Conversations continue. Advisors are consulted. Information is gathered. Yet no one is willing to make the decisions that would set a clear course. The family remains in perpetual preparation. Over time, this drift can harden into cynicism when family members no longer trust their own judgment or the guidance of others. Learning can become part of that inertia: "We need more data." "We need more time." Sometimes those instincts are prudent. At other times, they mask discomfort with responsibility.

Leadership breaks the freeze. Leadership in a family is not positional power. It is stewardship of momentum. It is the willingness to do the following:

- Clarify direction.
- Make decisions with incomplete information.
- Accept the discomfort of disagreement.
- Hold steady through transition.
- Act in service of long-term flourishing, even when short-term harmony is disturbed.

There is no standing still in a family system. Inaction is itself a choice, and it carries consequences. Momentum either builds or dissipates. Flourishing families do not eliminate uncertainty before acting. They cultivate leaders who can move forward within it. [42]

Architect of Opportunity

Some leaders build businesses. Some become stewards of wealth. A few evolve further: They become architects of opportunity. An architect of opportunity does not focus solely on preserving assets. Nor do they concentrate only on maintaining structure. They design conditions, and they ask questions such as:

Where will the next generation practice responsibility?
Where will they experiment safely?
Where will they fail and learn?
Where will they discover what they are capable of?

This kind of leadership differs from business-building and governance. Its work is not to control outcomes but to shape the environment in which families learn, decide, and grow. Architects of opportunity build pathways for growth. They create spaces for mentorship and role rotation. They encourage rising generations to teach what they are learning. They fund small experiments with real responsibility but contained risk. They make room for collaboration across branches, not because it is efficient but because it builds trust. They also pay attention to meaning. Shared purpose is translated into living practice in the form of rituals, gatherings, shared decisions, and participation guidelines. Values are not declared once; they are exercised repeatedly. Over time, these small, intentional investments compound. Confidence grows. Capability deepens. Relationships strengthen. Purpose becomes visible in action.

Financial capital, in this context, becomes fuel. Not the focus.

The architect understands that the most important inheritance is not money but readiness. And readiness does not emerge by accident.

Learning That Leads Somewhere

Learning, as we have used the term throughout this book, is not limited to formal education or financial literacy. It is the ongoing capacity to adapt, reflect, and integrate change without losing coherence. In families with economic capital, this capacity does not develop automatically. It must be supported.

Some families choose to make learning a visible priority. They create space for shared reflection, invite outside perspective, and designate people whose role is to support growth rather than enforce rules. Others keep learning informally, embedded in family rhythms rather than formal programs. Both approaches can work if they are aligned with the family's culture and values. The key choice is not between formal and informal. It is between accidental development and intentional development.

Lifelong Learning

Learning in later adulthood is just as vital as in earlier years, since elders play a unique and powerful role in sustaining a family's learning culture. When older family members continue to invest in their own growth, whether by seeking new knowledge, reflecting on life experience, or adapting to changing family dynamics, they model lifelong curiosity and humility. This ongoing commitment not only enriches their own lives but also signals to younger generations that learning is a lifelong journey, not a destination.

Elders who embrace learning become stewards of wisdom and adaptability, helping the family navigate transitions, honor the past, and remain open to the future. Their willingness to learn alongside others fosters intergenerational respect and keeps the family system vibrant and resilient. They build both internal and external capacity by leaning in with curiosity and driving learning curriculums tailored to each unique life stage.[43]

Gratitude, an Outcome of Learning

Gratitude is not something families can demand. It is often the byproduct of context, learning, and agency. A surprising outcome of intentional learning is gratitude[44]—not the performative gratitude that is demanded or expected, but the kind that grows from understanding. When family members are invited to understand the family's history and purpose, resources are no longer experienced as arbitrary windfalls or burdens. They are understood as part of a larger story.

Families sometimes worry about whether gratitude will follow from these choices. In our experience, gratitude cannot be required, but it can be recognized. When learning is supported, context is shared, and agency is respected, gratitude often appears—a signal that culture and care are aligned.

Many of the most persistent conflicts in families are not really about assets, roles, or decisions. They are about identity, voice, and respect. Because these concerns are abstract and deeply personal, they often masquerade as disputes over tangible issues. Learning-oriented families are better equipped to become curious about what conflict is signaling, rather than rushing to suppress it or resolve it prematurely.

Structures in Service of Culture

Some families, once clear on direction, choose to build structures that support their culture. Others remain informal. Structure should follow readiness. Often referred to as family governance, typical organizing bodies can range from informal gatherings to formal bodies with clearly articulated protocols, decision-making processes, and defined membership criteria.

On the informal end of the spectrum are learning gatherings, book clubs, mentoring relationships, coaching partnerships, learning cohorts, and support groups for family members navigating similar seasons of life, such as new parents, recent university graduates, or those experiencing loss. These casual family groups are flexible and adaptive. Participation may ebb and flow, with leadership roles often emerging organically as the structure evolves with the family's needs. Informal governance can be powerful precisely because it lowers the barrier to engagement and invites relational depth without procedural weight.

More formal governance structures introduce greater clarity and continuity as the number of family members increases. These may include family assemblies or family forums that gather the broader family periodically; family councils tasked with stewarding shared initiatives or articulating family values; generational forums that create space for peer-level learning and leadership development; or advisory boards composed of trusted outsiders invited to support the family's long-term development. Some families establish learning and development committees, philanthropy committees, or next-generation councils to focus on particular dimensions of growth. In others, a family office board or governance committee provides coordination between ownership, management, and family life.

We have encouraged some families to establish a Council of Elders. Unlike a family council, which may focus on coordination or decision-making, a Council of Elders is not primarily a governing body. Its purpose is less about authority and more rooted in wisdom. Elders are typically recognized for their lived experience, steadiness, and demonstrated commitment to the family's long-term flourishing. They serve as stewards of memory, meaning, and continuity, helping the family reflect on who it has been and who it hopes to become.

In moments of tension or uncertainty, they may offer perspective rather than directives, and guidance grounded in shared values rather than policy. When functioning well, a Council of Elders becomes a source of stability, reminding the family of its deeper purposes across generations. Elders do not replace trust fiduciaries or formal governance bodies; rather, they complement them by attending to the qualitative dimensions of family life that no legal structure can fully capture. In some families, these roles emerge gradually and are named only after they have proven useful. In others, they are designed intentionally from the outset. What matters is not the sophistication of the structure, but its fidelity to the family's purpose. Governance should support a living culture, not be a substitute for it.

Governance should support a living culture, not be a substitute for it.

When formal structures are introduced too early, or without sufficient cultural grounding, they often feel intrusive, controlling, or wasteful of time. When they are introduced thoughtfully, they can strengthen the family's capacity to grow and care for one another across generations.

Shared structures can intensify conflict rather than resolve it. Interdependence, overlapping roles, and power dynamics may amplify long-standing tensions, even when arrangements are well designed. The question is not whether shared structures will generate conflict, but whether the family has developed the cultural capacity to navigate it. Without that capacity, even sophisticated structures can become accelerants rather than stabilizers. Governance structures do not create unity, but they can create the conditions in which unity can be fostered. A forum can help to address disputes and differences that are completely natural and expected in families.[45]

Governance That Lives

The most effective structures are rarely permanent. They evolve as families evolve. What supports learning in one generation or season may become constraining in another. Often, family governance structures are best formed outside of the formal trust documents, with the trust documents providing funding of the family's learning and governance work. This may include support for hiring the qualitative specialist advisors to set up and facilitate these governance bodies to meet the family's needs. Legacy, in this sense, is not a fixed outcome to be secured once and preserved unchanged in formal legal form. It is iterative and re-visitable, shaped by ongoing dialogue, reflection, and adaptation.

Roles Families May Consider

Some families choose to name roles that support learning and development over time. These roles are not requirements or best practices. They are options families may adopt to fit their size, complexity, and aspirations. Not every family needs every role, and some roles can be combined or rotated.

Role *"Motto"*	**Description and Contribution**
Engaged Family Member *"Together we grow."*	Steps up and actively participates in creating the learning journey, along with supporting family life, learning, and decision-making. Includes roles of serving on the education, or learning and development, committee of the family council. At the pinnacle of service this family member becomes an "architect of opportunity." See page 102.
Responsible Beneficiary *"Receive with purpose; steward with care."*	Learns the trusts provisions, communicates proactively with trustees, builds financial literacy, aligns distributions with purpose and values, follows through on commitments, and develops capabilities over time.
Qualitative Trustee *"Steward with prudence; foster beneficiary well-being."*	Goes beyond the required baseline of carrying out grantor's intent, prudent administration, investments and distributions, to enhance beneficiary well being, learning and development. Asks the deeper questions and contributes to a culture of care.

Roles Families May Consider (cont.)

Role *"Motto"*	**Description and Contribution**
Observer *"See the whole."*	Listens deeply, reflects themes, and helps unlock impasses; if authorized by governance, may serve as narrow tiebreak fiduciary on a single issue.
Personne de Confiance[46] *"Comfortable being a great #2."*	Serves as a trusted confidant, advisor, or sounding board; fosters trust and emotional safety.
Elder[47] *"Wisdom lights the way."*	Provides wisdom, perspective, and continuity; models values and shares life lessons. An elder is not defined by age alone but by the willingness and ability to serve the family in these meaningful ways. Elders are stewards of the family's legacy, helping to guide and nurture future generations.
Chief Learning Officer *"Learning is our legacy."*	Designs and stewards the family's learning system across the five capitals; co-creates curricula, mentors rising gens, tracks readiness and progress.
Coach *"Build skills, unlock potential."*	Facilitates skillfully for growth, helping family members set goals, build capabilities, and run "safe-to-try" experiments; provides structure, feedback, and accountability (not therapy).

Roles Families May Consider (cont.)

Role *"Motto"*	**Description and Contribution**
Mentor *"Light their path; don't take their steps."*	Guides with experience, sharing lived wisdom; opens networks and models judgment and character over time through relationship.
Ghost *"Honor the past, inspire the future."*	Represents the influence and legacy of ancestors with a presence so strong that it impacts the family system currently. While ghosts can inspire reflection and connection to family history, balancing honor of the past while creating a pathway to create the future is key.
Historian/ Storyteller *"Stories shape culture; memory guides our future"*	Captures and curates the family's history, artifacts, and stories; maintains shared language; publishes minutes and decision rationales; and makes legacy materials accessible for learning across generations.

Learning Across the Whole Life of the Family

Families are often tempted to narrow learning to a single domain, often financial competence. While this is important, flourishing requires attention to the whole life of the family.

Learning takes different forms across different qualitative dimensions: human capacities such as self-knowledge and resilience; social capacities such as communication

Key Questions for the Four Intangible Capitals[48]

Human Capital	Spiritual Capital
Well-being of each family member (mental, emotional, and physical); ability to flourish as individuals Ability of each to contribute meaningfully to their lives and the family system	Meaning and shared purpose Ability to inspire family members across generations to be part of the family Uniting in a way that transcends mere biological or legal relationships
Is every member engaged in meaningful productivity, striving to achieve his or her highest purpose to bring their own dream to life? Are they attending to physical and psychological well-being?	Does the family have a shared transcendent purpose? Has each member integrated the meaning of true wealth in their life? Does the family recognize its connection to each other and the greater world?
The most significant asset on the balance sheet is the family members themselves. Measured by the flourishing of every family member, their family relationships, and contributions to the collective well-being of the family.	Often grounded in an intention to enhance the journeys of each member toward the whole family thriving. Active practice of gratitude and humility. Balancing love and power. Balancing independence and interdependence.

Key Questions (cont.)

Social Capital	Intellectual Capital
Communication and collaboration (including thoughtful shared decision-making) Ability to welcome new members Giving time, talent, and treasure to the larger society	Emotional Intelligence, curiosity, and critical thinking Acquiring, creating, and passing on knowledge Integrating learning into action
Does the family make timely decisions under pressure (both internal and external)? Does the family have the capacity to constructively work through differences? How does the family actively show care to their community?	Is the family a perpetual learning system—seeking feedback, stretching and drawing on the unique gifts of each member? Does the family focus on vertical development, expanding the original container itself (i.e., increasing capacity) along with horizontal development?
This starts with the family's ability to make decisions and broadens to the family's ability to extend their reach to be in service of something bigger than themselves.	The family's ability to acquire new knowledge, share it among its members, and then, most importantly, integrate it into its behaviors and competencies is the true measure of a learning system.

and collaboration; intellectual capacities such as curiosity and critical thinking; spiritual capacities such as meaning and purpose. Included in this learning is an understanding of the nature and respective responsibilities of the trustee-beneficiary relationship, which is vital to fostering a qualitative connection between these roles.

Returning to the idea proposed in chapter 2, consider setting out a share of the financial assets in a trust or pool to create a source of funding for the investment needed to grow the family as a whole (a "well-being share").

Families who attend to learning across these dimensions are better equipped to navigate complexity without becoming brittle. They are less likely to confuse success with compliance or freedom with carelessness.

Maddie, Choosing Forward

For Maddie, the movement from understanding to action became real when she and Omar decided to redo their own estate plans.

The originals had been prepared years earlier, at the strong urging of the trustee, and they reflected the mindset Maddie had come to know so well: names, percentages, distribution language, taxes, contingencies. Efficient, orderly, and emotionally vacant. The documents said nothing about the character of the family Maddie and Omar hoped to build, nothing about the purpose of the resources, and nothing about how future relationships might be welcomed and sustained.

By then, Maddie had done her homework. After months of quiet inquiry, she found an estate planning attorney whose approach felt entirely different. Before their first substantive meeting, the attorney sent a questionnaire. It did ask about children, trustees, and assets, but it also asked deeper questions:

- What do you hope this planning will make possible in the lives of your children?

- What intention and values do you want them to understand when they encounter these documents one day in the future?

- If the trust were given a name with meaning for your family, what would it be?

- What do you want those who join your family to experience when they become a member?

That evening, after the children were asleep, Maddie and Omar sat down at the kitchen table with the questionnaire between them.

At first, they moved slowly. They talked about the practical matters, then paused over the questions that felt less familiar. When Maddie read aloud, "What do you want those who join your family to experience when they become a member?" she stopped.

Omar looked at the page for a long moment before answering.

"I think they should feel welcomed before they feel evaluated," he said.

Maddie knew immediately what he meant. He was not speaking about a single incident. He was naming a pattern that had shaped his experience with her family from the beginning. Her family had not made it easy to belong. There had been caution where there might have been warmth. Scrutiny where there might have been curiosity. The money was never openly discussed, yet it hovered over everything. He had entered not simply a family but a guarded system, and for a long time he had the distinct sense that he was being measured against standards no one would name. Omar reminded Maddie of some of the more painful encounters he had tucked away in memories but which still stung as he recounted them.

As she listened, Maddie felt something settle into focus. She had spent years understanding the trust as a beneficiary. Now she could see more clearly what it had felt like from the outside, for the person who had chosen her and then had to find his place inside a family shaped by silence, judgment, hierarchy, and inherited caution.

The conversation changed. They stopped talking about what they would leave and began talking about what kind of life they wanted to create for their children and their children's partners. They asked themselves what they should be explaining early rather than withholding, to be learned someday from an attorney. They focused on how a future son- or daughter-in-law might be brought into family conversations without being tested first. How a structure could protect without casting suspicion. How money could be named without becoming the center of the family's identity.

By the end of the evening, the questionnaire had become something more than a planning tool. It had opened a different kind of authorship. Maddie and Omar were not merely preparing documents. They were deciding how they would live and what they wished their children would inherit beyond assets: curiosity, compassion, a sense of stewardship, a desire to welcome, agency.

When they met with the attorney, they came ready with a carefully thought-out set of priorities. They were focused on creating a plan that reflected intention and care as well as technical competence. They would work for clarity without rigidity, guidance without overreach, and enough humanity in the language that their children might one day recognize not only instructions but also hear their voices as well as understand their intention. Most of all, they wanted to leave behind a structure their family could live in, one that would enhance their lives—not one they would have to struggle within.

For Maddie, that process felt entirely different from what had shaped her earlier life. It did not begin with control. It began with questions. It made room for memory, for judgment, for regret, and for hope. It felt less like submitting to a structure and more like taking responsibility for one.

The trust she had inherited had not changed. But now it no longer stood as the only model available to her. It had become one part of her history, not the template for her future.

Her story does not end with resolution or certainty. It ends with choice.

No Single Model, Only Responsible Choice

It is tempting, at this point, to offer a model to follow or a checklist to complete. We have resisted that impulse throughout this book, not because models are unhelpful, but because flourishing cannot be standardized without losing what makes it alive. Families differ—their histories, values, and capacities. Responsible choice requires attention to those differences.

Flourishing families, and the advisors who serve them, approach this work with humility and curiosity rather than certainty. They recognize that no plan, structure, or model can anticipate every future, and that learning together over time is more reliable than conviction locked into documents.

Families rarely grow beyond conflict by winning arguments or enforcing solutions. They grow by developing greater capacity, individually and collectively. This developmental approach does not promise harmony or agreement. It offers something more durable: the ability to stay in dialogue, revisiting assumptions, and continuing to grow together even when differences persist.

Understanding is not the finish line. At some point, each family must move to decision: to decide what it will fund, tolerate, and prioritize, and who will lead. Flourishing is not secured by insight alone, but by disciplined, repeated choice.

Choosing How to Live

In the end, every family must answer the same question: How then shall we live?

The answer will not be found in a trust instrument or a balance sheet. It will be found in daily decisions, in relationships sustained over time, and in the willingness to remain curious, caring, and accountable across generations.

At this point, no framework or example can substitute for your own judgment. Only you can decide what intentional living will look like for your family, and what you are willing to invest to support it.

When families decide with intention, they experience themselves as authors of their shared life, and the work feels lighter, even when it remains serious.

Flourishing, understood as the true measure of wealth, is not inherited. It is practiced, one choice at a time. And then, if we are thoughtful, fortunate, and intentional, we pass it on.

Do the best you can until you know better.
Then when you know better, do better.

Maya Angelou

Now Choose

- ❍ What's one conversation your family keeps *almost* having—but hasn't quite? What would it take to actually have it?

- ❍ If you embrace your role as a co-author of your family's story—not just a character in it—what's one thing you will write differently?

- ❍ Where in your family's life might *learning* be functioning as a way to avoid *deciding*? What would action actually look like?

- ❍ What's the smallest, most concrete step you could take this year to move your family toward flourishing? (Not the most ambitious—the most *doable*.)

- ❍ Who in your family has been an architect of opportunity? How might you build pathways for the growth of family members?

- ❍ Consider this sentence together, as a family: "We each welcome you to our family with an open heart, mind, and will, and with deep appreciation for your choosing us." Does it feel true for everyone? What would have to change for it to feel completely true?

- ❍ What do you want the rising generation to say about this season of your family's life, 30 years from now?

From Insight to Action: What is your key takeaway?

"The play's the thing."
Shakespeare, *Hamlet*

Well-Being Lexicon

About this lexicon. This lexicon is a quick reference to the ideas that shape *Family Flourishing*. It is meant to give families a shared language for talking about wealth as well-being, and for asking how planning, trusts, and family culture can enhance real lives. Use it to pause, align, and keep moving one thoughtful step at a time toward a flourishing family.

Wealth as Well-being

Wealth (as Well-being)
Wealth is not money alone; it is well-being. In this book, wealth means the conditions that allow people to grow, connect, contribute, find meaning, and live with health and dignity over time. We use "financial wealth" or "economic wealth" to discuss money or assets.

Well-being
Well-being is how a life is actually lived and felt—mentally, emotionally, physically, relationally, and spiritually. A family can preserve assets flawlessly and still lose the people and relationships those assets were meant to support.

Flourishing

Flourishing is well-being over time. It includes growth, health, meaning, character, contribution, and connection. It is not the same as comfort or consumption. A flourishing family creates conditions in which each person can develop, belong, and contribute to flourishing societies across generations. It is a way of seeing that each family interprets and lives for itself.

The Five Capitals

The Five Capitals are a fuller map of family wealth. Financial capital is only one form of capital. The other four—human, intellectual, social, and spiritual—are qualitative. They help determine whether money becomes a gift or a burden.

- **Human Capital.** The well-being and capabilities of each family member: health, maturity, resilience, self-knowledge, purpose, and the ability to do meaningful work. Human capital is what makes stewardship possible.

- **Intellectual Capital.** The family's capacity to learn, think, adapt, and apply wisdom. Intellectual capital includes curiosity, critical thinking, shared knowledge, and the ability to turn learning into action.

- **Social Capital.** The strength of the family's relationships. It includes trust, communication, collaboration, conflict resilience, shared decision-making, the ability to welcome new members into the life of the family and to contribute to the community in which the family lives.

- **Spiritual Capital (or Legacy Capital).** Shared meaning and purpose—what the family stands for and serves beyond itself. Spiritual capital is not doctrine or a required belief. It is the lived orientation and practice that gives coherence and direction across generations.

- **Financial Capital.** Money and assets: measurable, portable, and powerful. In this book, financial capital is fuel, not the finish line. Its highest purpose is to serve human, intellectual, social, and spiritual flourishing.

The Qualitative Lens

A qualitative lens asks how a plan, trust, decision, or family habit will be experienced by real people. It does not reject technical excellence. It widens the view so structure serves life, relationship, learning, and purpose.

Inheritance, Estate Planning, and Trusts

Wealth Transfer

The movement of wealth from one generation to another. It is never only financial. It can shape identity, belonging, responsibility, family relationships, and a person's sense of freedom or obligation.

The Meteor Effect

A large inheritance or gift can land like a meteor: sudden, forceful, disorienting, and difficult to integrate. Preparation, shared language, and family culture can prepare the inheritor for the impact and transform its arrival into a life-enhancing gift.

The Big Reveal

The moment a family member learns the size, complexity, and constraints of the family's financial wealth all at once—often late, in a formal office, and without enough context. Families may intend protection and privacy, but the experience can create shock, confusion, or powerlessness.

Estate Plan

The legal plan for how property, responsibility, and decision-making will be handled during life, at death, and often long after death. This book looks beyond the technical provisions of the estate plan to promote drafting that ensures the structure creates the conditions that future family members can live, and play, within.

Qualitative Estate Plan

An estate plan designed to enhance lives, not only protect assets. It begins with the human why: How will this plan support development, relationships, belonging, purpose, and flourishing over time?

Trust
A trust is an arrangement in which one person or institution holds and manages property for the benefit of another person or group. A trust is a legal structure, but it is also something people experience in daily life.

Trust Creator
The person who creates a trust and places property into it, usually with hopes about how the trust will serve descendants. Legal documents may use words such as grantor, settlor, or donor. We use trust creator because it keeps attention on authorship, intention, and care.

Beneficiary
A person for whose benefit a trust is held. A beneficiary is not merely a recipient of money. A beneficiary is a human being whose life, relationships, and sense of agency may be shaped by the trust.

Trustee
The person or institution entrusted to administer a trust. A trustee must manage assets responsibly, follow the trust document, and account to beneficiaries. In a qualitative relationship, the trustee also pays attention to whether the trust is enhancing lives.

Fiduciary
Someone who holds power for the benefit of another and must act with loyalty, care, and accountability. Trustees are fiduciaries. The word can sound technical, but at heart it means power held in service.

Trust as a Human Relationship

A trust is relational before it is legal. One person holds authority and responsibility for the benefit of another. The quality of the trustee-beneficiary relationship often determines whether the trust feels like care, control, support, or constraint.

Gift of Love Intention

A simple statement in a trust preamble that the trust is a gift of love intended to enhance the lives of the beneficiaries. This language sets a human tone and reminds trustees that the trust exists to serve people, not only property.

Letter of Wishes

A non-binding letter written to the trustee that explains the trust creator's values, hopes, priorities, and guidance. It gives human context to legal language and helps trustees administer with wisdom rather than guesswork.

Legacy Letter (Ethical Will or Love Letter)

A message to descendants that shares stories, values, hopes, lessons, and blessings. It is less about instructions and more about meaning—what the writer wants family members to understand about life, not just assets.

Flexibility (Both/And Design)

A good plan balances structure and adaptability: enough clarity to guide, enough room to evolve. Flexible planning recognizes that future people, cultures, laws, and needs cannot be fully known today.

Way Back Home (Redemption Path)
A design principle that avoids permanent exclusion with no path to repair. Families can hold boundaries and still leave room for growth, forgiveness, healing, and renewed belonging.

Well-being Share (Family Share)
A pool of resources set aside for the family as a whole. It may support gatherings and learning, and help with conflict-resolution, shared philanthropy, or other practices that strengthen connection across branches.

Incentive Trust
A trust that ties distributions to specific behaviors or milestones, such as education, employment, or other achievements. These provisions often begin with good intentions, but overly rigid incentives can send a message that support is conditional and may not build the qualities families hope for.

Pot Trust (Shared Trust)
A trust that holds assets for several beneficiaries together rather than in separate shares. It can be useful, but without clarity and care it may create competition, confusion, or resentment about who receives what and when.

Perpetual or Dynasty Trust
A trust designed to last for many generations, and in some cases indefinitely. The longer a trust may last, the more important it becomes to build in flexibility, human purpose, and a culture of care.

Trust Administration and the People It Serves

Qualitative Trust Administration
Trust administration that treats the trust as a lived experience, not only paperwork. It is the pattern of decisions, conversations, discretion, learning, and care that determines whether a trust supports or constrains a beneficiary's life.

Accounting to the Beneficiary
More than sending statements or reports. At its best, accounting means the trustee helps the beneficiary understand the trust relationship and is answerable for whether the trust is serving its highest purpose: enhancing the beneficiary's life.

Autonomy and Agency
The ability to make meaningful choices and act with responsibility. Trusts can either strengthen agency by inviting learning and participation, or weaken it by creating dependency and silence.

The Moral Gap
The gap created when one person receives benefits from property but does not hold the legal authority or day-to-day responsibility for it. A qualitative trust relationship helps close this gap through learning, accountability, and shared purpose.

Entropic Drift

The slow loss of energy, purpose, and responsibility that can happen when financial capital is preserved but human development is not cultivated. Families counter this drift through learning, contribution, and meaningful roles.

Beneficiary Relations Committee

A group designed to keep attention on the human impact of the trust. It may support distributions, mentoring, beneficiary learning, and the quality of engagement between trustees and beneficiaries.

Qualitative Trustee

A trustee who meets the technical duties of trusteeship and also brings humility, curiosity, emotional steadiness, and attention to beneficiary well-being. A qualitative trustee stewards beneficiaries as well as property.

Responsible Beneficiary

A beneficiary who learns about the trust, communicates with purpose, follows through on commitments, and uses resources in ways that support their growth, contribution, and well-being.

Private Trust Company (PTC)

A family-created company that serves as trustee for family trusts. A PTC can support continuity, learning, and family engagement when the family is prepared to invest in governance, talent, and care. It can also magnify problems if used only as a technical administrative device.

Family Culture and Choice

Qualitative Family Culture
The lived habits, values, relationships, and practices that shape how a family handles money, difference, responsibility, belonging, and change. A qualitative family culture is what allows estate planning and trusts to become life-enhancing.

Culture of Care
A family posture that attends to real people in real seasons of life. Care is not softness or avoidance. It combines love, boundaries, accountability, and the willingness to stay engaged when things are difficult.

Family Governance
The ways a family organizes shared learning, communication, decisions, roles, and responsibilities. Governance may be informal or formal. It works best when it supports a living culture rather than replacing one.

Elder
A family member or trusted person recognized not by age alone, but by steadiness, lived wisdom, humility, and willingness to serve the family's long-term flourishing.

Council of Elders
A wisdom-centered group whose purpose is not command and control, but stewardship of memory, meaning, and continuity. Elders offer perspective and values-based guidance while complementing, not replacing, trustees or formal governance bodies.

Personne de Confiance

A trusted confidant or sounding board who helps create emotional safety and perspective. This person is often comfortable being a wise number two rather than the person in charge.

Architect of Opportunity

A family leader who creates places for others to practice responsibility, learn, experiment safely, fail thoughtfully, and discover what they are capable of becoming.

Chief Learning Officer

A person or role that helps steward the family's learning across the Five Capitals. The work may include learning plans, mentors, gatherings, curricula, and ways to track growth over time.

Ghost

An unintegrated past influence - an excluded person, ungrieved loss, secret, unresolved conflict, or trauma - that shapes the family indirectly, surfacing as silence, tension, repeating conflict, or rigid loyalty to old rules, and calling the family to name and integrate it.

Learning as Adaptation

Learning is self-initiated change. It includes gaining knowledge, but also unlearning old assumptions, listening for what life is showing now, and adapting without losing coherence. Learning is a lifelong journey.

Welcoming and Belonging

Belonging is not inherited automatically. It is offered, received, and renewed. A welcoming family sees spouses, partners, in-laws, and future generations not as threats to be tested, but as people choosing the family and bringing their own gifts.

Open Mind, Open Heart, and Open Will

A welcoming practice of suspending judgment, approaching others with compassion, and having the courage to let the family's identity grow as new people and new realities enter. Inspired by Otto Scharmer.

Play

Play is not frivolous. It is how people practice, experiment, connect, and learn without fear taking over. Families that can play often stay more flexible, engaged, and alive across generations.

Gratitude Letter

A practice in which a beneficiary names how a gift, trust, or family resource has affected their life and what they have learned from it. Gratitude grows best from understanding and agency, not from being demanded.

References

Endnotes and Further Learning

The following sources support and inform the material presented in each chapter, while the Resources for Further Learning extend an invitation for deeper exploration and reflection.

Preamble and Chapter 1 Endnotes

1 *Shorter Oxford English Dictionary*, 5th ed., vol. 2 (2002), under "weal."

2 *Shorter Oxford English Dictionary*, 5th ed., vol. 2 (2002), under "wealth."

3 "Artistotle's Ethics," *Stanford Encyclopedia of Philosophy*, last revised July 2, 2022, https://plato.stanford.edu/entries/aristotle-ethics/.

4 Among models for flourishing are Maslow's hierarchy of needs, Gallup's elements of well-being based on the Cantril Ladder, the Flourishing Scale (FS), the OECD scale, and Martin Seligman's PERMA model of positive psychology and his framework for well-being.

5 The Cornell Family Estrangement and Reconciliation Project is a research initiative led by sociologist and gerontologist Karl Pillemer at Cornell University. It was established to investigate the causes, consequences, and potential resolutions of family estrangement.

6 Karl Pillemer, *Fault Lines: Fractured Families and How to Mend Them* (Avery, 2020); Pillemer, K., Suitor, J. J., Riffin, C., & Gilligan, M. (2020). "Mothers and Their Adult Children: A Mixed-Methods Study of Intergenerational Relationships and Estrangement." *Journal of Marriage and Family*, 82(2), 783–800.

7 The analogy of the meteor was developed by James E. Hughes Jr. See James E. Hughes Jr., Susan E. Massenzio, and Keith Whitaker, *The Cycle of the Gift: Family Wealth and Wisdom* (Bloomberg Press, 2012).

8 Many firms are discussing this topic, including Boston Consulting Group (*Global Wealth 2021*), Cerulli Associates (2020), and Accenture (2014), The Great Wealth Transfer: Securing Your Legacy in a Changing World. The James E. Hughes Jr. Foundation, in partnership with Peter Moustakerski, CEO of Family Office Exchange, is gathering 200 practitioners from around the world to explore the Great Wealth Transfer (GWT). This 100 Year Committee for Family and Societal Flourishing is examining the forces of the GWT and the realities of demographic decline to explore their impact on families, communities and broader society. See also: John J. Havens and Paul G. Schervish, *A Golden Age of Philanthropy? The Impact of the Great Wealth Transfer on Greater Boston* (The Boston Foundation, 2006).

9 Hughes, Jr., et al., *The Cycle of the Gift*.

10 See James E. Hughes Jr., *Family Wealth: Keeping It in the Family - How Family Members and Their Advisers Preserve Human, Intellectual, and Financial Assets for Generations* (Bloomberg Press, 2004).

Chapter 1 Resources for Further Learning

- Hughes, James E., Jr. *Family Wealth: Keeping It in the Family - How Family Members and Their Advisers Preserve Human, Intellectual, and Financial Assets for Generations*. Bloomberg Press, 2004.

- Hughes, James E., Jr., Susan E. Massenzio, and Keith Whitaker. *Complete Family Wealth: Wealth as Well-Being.* 2nd ed. Bloomberg Press, 2022.
- Hughes, James E., Jr. and Peter Moustakerski. Foxcast CEO Series: *Rediscovering the Meaning of Wealth—as Wellbeing.*

  https://www.familyoffice.com/podcasts/Rediscovering-the-Meaning-of-Wealth%E2%80%93as-Wellbeing, Jun 28, 2023.
- Michiels, Anneleen, and Claudia Astrachan. *It's (Not) All About the Money: The Many Misunderstood and Underexplored Manifestations of Money in the Business Family.* Generation6, 2023. https://www.generation6.com/research.
- Miller, Lisa, and James E. Hughes Jr. "Spiritual Capital: The Foundation for Flourishing Families." The James E. Hughes Jr. Foundation, November 7, 2025. YouTube, 10 min., 30 sec. https://www.youtube.com/watch?v=49Hj36J-DxE.
- Mutendi, Tsitsi. *Raising the Baobab: A Collection of Tools for Multigenerational Wealth Building in Family Businesses*. Published by the author, 2024.
- Polk, Ken. *The Spirit of Wealth Preservation: Leverage Your Finite Life for the Infinite Good*. Forbes Books, 2025.

Chapter 2 Endnotes

11 Building on James E. Hughes Jr. and Keith Whitaker, "The Often Unexpected Consequences of the Creation of a Perpetual Trust," January 1, 2025.

12 James Grubman, with foreword by Dennis T. Jaffe, *Strangers in Paradise: How Families Adapt to Wealth Across Generations* (pub. by author, 2013).

13 Michele Mikeska, "Creating Balance in Financially Diverse Partnerships When She Has the Money," *Trusts & Estates*, May 21, 2020, Wealth Management, https://www.wealthmanagement.com/estate-planning/creating-balance-in-financially-diverse-partnerships-when-she-has-the-money.

14 While people tend to have a mindset preference of either "promotion" (focus on opportunity, advancement, aspiration, and gains) or "prevention" (vigilance, security, responsibility, and the avoidance of loss), both promotion and prevention orientations are necessary for long-term success. These ideas originated from E. Tory Higgins and were evolved by his student, Heidi Grant Halvorson. Stacy Allred brings this idea to life by wearing a double-sided cape in family meetings (custom made on Etsy) and leveraging the ideas of James O. Pawelski (Positive Psychology Center, University of Pennsylvania). Each family member is asked to self-identify which type of superhero they are: red-cape superhero—keep out the bad—or green-cape superhero—let in the good—then we reinforce the importance of embracing both/and by broadening access to both sides of the double-sided cape.

15 Scotty McLennan, "Creating an Ethical Will," in *Wealth of Wisdom: Top Practices for Wealthy Families and Their Advisors*, ed. Tom McCullough and Keith Whitaker (Wiley, 2022), chap. 27.

16 See "Letter of Wishes Example" along with "Sample Statement of Grantor Intent for and Wishes for Beneficiaries" plus other resources at "Resources," Beneficiary Thriving, accessed April 27, 2026, https://www.beneficiarythriving.com/resources.

17 John A. Warnick's Purposeful Planning Approach emphasizes creating gift and estate plans that go beyond the transfer of financial assets to include family values, relationships, and legacy. Warnick encourages families to engage in open dialogue, intentional decision-making, and the integration of personal meaning and purpose into their planning processes. "Guidelights" are the core values, intentions, wisdom-based guidance, and shared principles in a family, meant to illuminate, not dictate. The idea is to enrich the lives of beneficiaries by drawing on a lifetime of accumulated wisdom and experience, functioning as a non-binding framework that helps beneficiaries and trustees navigate decisions and life challenges with clarity about the grantor's deeper values and priorities. See John A. Warnick, "Articles & Papers," Purposeful Planning Institute, accessed May 3, 2026, https://purposefulplanninginstitute.com/articles-papers/. See also John A. Warnick, "Achieving Purpose Through Family Traditions With John A. Warnick," *FOXcast*, podcast audio, April 16, 2024, https://podcasts.apple.com/us/podcast/achieving-purpose-through-family-traditions-with-john/id1459145496?i=1000761837105.

18 For further learning, see Hartley Goldstone, James E. Hughes Jr., and Keith Whitaker, "Creating Preambles," chap. 10 and "Sample Legacy Letter," appendix 1 in *Family Trusts: A Guide for Beneficiaries, Trustees, Trust Protectors, and Trust Creators* (Wiley, 2016).

19 I met a traveller from an antique land
Who said: Two vast and trunkless legs of stone
Stand in the desart.[sic] Near them, on the sand,
Half sunk, a shattered visage lies, whose frown,
And wrinkled lip, and sneer of cold command,
Tell that its sculptor well those passions read
Which yet survive, stamped on these lifeless things,
The hand that mocked them, and the heart that fed:
And on the pedestal these words appear:
"My name is Ozymandias, King of Kings:
Look on my works, ye Mighty, and despair!"

Nothing beside remains. Round the decay
Of that colossal Wreck, boundless and bare
The lone and level sands stretch far away.
—*Percy Shelley*, "Ozymandias," *1819*

20 An example of a polarity, a set of interdependent and seemingly opposite pairs that need to be balanced, rather than a problem to be solved, is: Inhale, Exhale. One doesn't exist without the other. While a deeper discussion on managing polarities is beyond the scope of this book, we encourage you to explore this powerful concept further. An excellent resource is Cathy Carroll, *Hug of War: How to Lead a Family Business with Both Love and Logic* (Koehler Books, 2024).

21 Adam Kahane, *Power and Love: A Theory and Practice of Social Change*, illustrated by Jeff Barnum (Berrett-Koehler, 2010).

22 Consider including trust language that empowers trustees to engage directly (or reimburse beneficiaries for) a broad range of specialist advisors with the goal of proactively supporting trustees' well-being. In addition to including the typical advisors of lawyers and tax and investment professionals, build flexibility to include counselors; clinical psychologists; coaches; mediators; experts in the fields of family dynamics, family emotional systems, learning and development (across different life stages: childhood, teen, adult); and health and wellness professionals (including alternative medicine practitioners, trauma experts, psychiatrists, mental health practitioners, nutritional experts, psychotherapists, marriage counselors, couples therapists, and family systems therapists).

23 While incentives can boost performance on simple or mechanical tasks, they frequently undermine intrinsic motivation, creativity, and judgment in complex work—reducing performance when the task requires cognitive flexibility or deep problem solving. See Dan Ariely et al., "Large Stakes and Big Mistakes," *Review of Economic Studies* 76, no. 2 (2009): 451–469, https://academic.oup.com/restud/article-abstract/76/2/451/1594205. Regarding financial incentives in

estate planning, see Jon J. Gallo, Eileen Gallo, and James Grubman, "The Use and Abuse of Incentive Trusts: Improvements and Alternatives," presentation, 45th Annual Heckerling Institute on Estate Planning, Orlando, January 2011. The authors note that incentive provisions often reflect the grantor's values and fears more than the beneficiary's needs and motivations, and they can unintentionally undermine development rather than support it. Their critical examination of incentive trust structures challenged conventional assumptions about whether monetary incentives effectively motivate desired behaviors in beneficiaries. Drawing on contemporary motivational psychology research and management theory, the authors demonstrate that traditional incentive trusts often fail to achieve their intended objectives and propose results-oriented alternatives that emphasize discretionary distributions guided by clear mission statements and trustee guidelines rather than rigid, behavior-contingent provisions. See also Gallo, Gallo, Grubman, "Not Your Typical Incentive Trust: The ROTE and FST, Parts 1 and 2," *Journal of Financial Planning*, April 2011, https://jamesgrubman.com/wp-content/uploads/1620/65/Not_Your_Typical_Incentive_Tru_and_FST_Part_I_JFP_April_2011-pg-1.pdf and https://jamesgrubman.com/wp-content/uploads/1620/65/Not_Your_Typical_Incentive_Trust_The_ROTE_and_FST_Part_II_JFP_April_2011.pdf, accessed May 3, 2026.

24 Todd A. Flubacher et al., "Delaware's New Beneficiary Well-Being Statute," *Trusts & Estates*, January 2025, 34–39.

25 A growing field of professionals can support a family in this work to articulate the human "why" before the attorney addresses the legal "how." Relevant advisors range from family governance consultants to leadership coaches; all require strong facilitation skills.

Chapter 2 Resources for Further Learning

- Allred, Stacy, Mary Duke, and James E. Hughes Jr. "Can Your Client's Family Live in the Estate Plan You Create?" *Trusts & Estates*, December 2022.
- Arnold, Elizabeth. *Creating the Good Will: The Most Comprehensive Guide to Both the Financial and Emotional Sides of Passing on Your Legacy*. Portfolio, 2006.
- Baris, Mitchell, Carla Garrity, Carol Warnick, and John Warnick. "Maturity Markers: A New Paradigm for Trust Distribution Models and Gifting Strategies." Family Firm Institute (FFI). Updated 2008. https://purposefulplanninginstitute.com/wp-content/uploads/2023/02/Maturity-Markers-A-New-Paradigm-for-Trust-Distribution-Models-and-Gifting.pdf.
- Harrison, Louis S., Kim Kamin, and Martin M. Shenkman. "The Gumby Trust: Creating Flexibility." *Trusts & Estates*, October 2018, 18–31. Thinking continues to evolve on creating flexible trusts, including Kamin's presentation at Purposeful Planning Institute's Symposium, February 11-13, 2026.
- Kamin, Kim, Avi Z. Kestenbaum, and Elliot Dizon. "Unequal Inheritances: A Final Parental Communication." *Trusts & Estates*, February 2021.
- McLennan, Scotty. "Creating an Ethical Will." *Wealth of Wisdom Podcast*. Hosted by Tom McCullough. Episode 88, November 21, 2023. https://www.wealthofwisdombook.com/podcast/88. Also "Creating an Ethical Will." In *Wealth of Wisdom: Top Practices for Wealthy Families and Their Advisors*, edited by Tom

McCullough and Keith Whitaker. Wiley, 2022. McLennan shares how after thinking about it for a few years, he went into the garden and focused for 30 minutes, drafting an ethical will and sharing it with his sons on his 70th birthday; he provides a framework for others to create their own ethical will.

- Warnick, John A., is a thought leader on creating more holistic estate documents. See "Expressing Purpose in Your Trusts." In *Wealth of Wisdom: Top Practices for Wealthy Families and Their Advisors*, edited by Tom McCullough and Keith Whitaker. Wiley, 2022.
- Wesley, Matthew. "The Hidden Truth About Values." Hidden Gem #8. The James E. Hughes Jr. Foundation, revised 2023. https://jehjf.org/hidden-gem-8-the-hidden-truth-about-values/.

Chapter 3 Endnotes

26 Daniel P. Felix, *The Way of the Trustee: A Holistic Guide to Enlightened Trust Administration in Service to Families* (James E. Hughes Jr. Foundation Publishing, 2024).

27 For further exploration, see the two-part article series by James E. Hughes Jr., and Keith Whitaker, "On Accounting to the Beneficiary," *FFI Practitioner*, November 19, 2025, https://digital.ffi.org/editions/on-accounting-to-the-beneficiary/ and "Building a Culture of Care in Trusts," *FFI Practitioner*, June 4, 2025, https://digital.ffi.org/building-a-culture-of-care-in-trusts-part-i/.

28 For a collection of positive stories of what's possible with qualitative trust administration, see Hartley Goldstone and Kathy Wiseman, *TrustWorthy: New Angles on Trusts from Beneficiaries and Trustees* (CreateSpace, 2012). The authors capture exemplar beneficiary/trustee relationships that support beneficiaries successfully integrating inheritances into their lives.

29 See also Hartley Goldstone, James E. Hughes Jr., and Keith Whitaker, "Private Trust Companies," appendix 4 in *Family Trusts: A Guide for Beneficiaries, Trustees, Trust Protectors, and Trust Creators* (Wiley, 2016).

Chapter 3 Resources for Further Learning

- Angus, Patricia M. *The Trustee Primer: A Guide for Personal Trustees*. Angus Advisory Group, 2015.
- Felix, Daniel P. *The Way of the Trustee: A Holistic Guide to Enlightened Trust Administration in Service to Families*. James E. Hughes Jr. Foundation Publishing, 2024.
- Goldstone, Hartley, James E. Hughes Jr., and Keith Whitaker. *Family Trusts: A Guide for Beneficiaries, Trustees, Trust Protectors, and Trust Creators*. Wiley, 2016.
- Goldstone, Hartley, and Kathy Wiseman. *TrustWorthy: New Angles on Trusts from Beneficiaries and Trustees*. CreateSpace, 2012.
- Hughes, James E. Jr., and Keith Whitaker. "The First Trustee," *FFI Practitioner*, February 4, 2026.
- Hughes, James E. Jr., and Vaughan Scott. "Trustee Versus Trustee—A Critical Distinction in Supporting Good Joint Decision-Making." Axiom Financial Strategies Group. Accessed April 27, 2026. https://www.axiomfsg.com/trustee-versus-trustee-a-critical-distinction-in-supporting-good-joint-decision-making/.
- Koplin, Amanda, Marin M. Shenkman, and Richard Trumpler. "Working with Beneficiaries with Mental

Health Challenges, an Action Plan for Estate Planners and Trustees." Steve Leimberg's Estate Planning Newsletter, February 3, 2025.

- Kotter, John P. *Leading Change*. Harvard Business Review Press, 2012.
- Marcus, George E., with Peter Dobkin Hall. *Lives in Trust: The Fortunes of Dynastic Families in Late Twentieth-Century America*. Westview Press, 1992.
- McCloskey, Jennifer Zelvin, "A Trust Without Funding Is Just Paper: Avoid These Common Mistakes." Alumni & Friends. University of Delaware. Accessed January 23, 2026. https://www.udel.edu/alumni-friends/stories/2025/pitfalls-of-not-funding-trust/. McCloskey is the founding director for the Trust Management minor at the University of Delaware. This program focuses on building the qualitative skills, along with the technical skills, that create more holistic trustee mindsets.
- Peppet, Scott. "Distribution Challenges from the Perspective of a Responsible Adult Beneficiary." Scott Peppet. Accessed January 22, 2026. https://scottpeppet.com/articles/for-family-members/distribution-challenges-from-the-perspective-of-a-responsible-adult-beneficiary/.
- Walsh, Judy Lin, and Stephen Salley. "The Inheritance Effect." *Trusts & Estates*, August 2020.
- Warnick, John A. "Generative Trusts and Trustees: A New Paradigm for Design and Administration." *Trusts & Estates*, April 23, 2018. https://www.wealthmanagement.com/estate-planning/generative-trusts-and-trustees.

Chapter 4 Endnotes

30 Matthew Wesley, "The Blob: How Culture Eats Structure for Breakfast," Hidden Gem #3, The James E. Hughes Jr. Foundation, accessed April 25, 2026, https://jehjf.org/the-blob-how-culture-eats-structure-for-breakfast/.

31 Brené Brown, *Braving the Wilderness: The Quest for True Belonging and the Courage to Stand Alone* (Random House, 2017), 31.

32 C. Otto Scharmer, Katrin Kaufer, *Presencing: 7 Practices for Transforming Self, Society, and Business* (Berrett-Koehler Publishers, 2025). See also Scharmer's earlier work *Theory U: Leading from the Future as It Emerges* (Berrett-Koehler Publishers, 2009); "Leading from the Emerging Future," Presencing Institute, accessed April 25, 2026, https://www.presencing.org/.

33 See Dennis T. Jaffe, *Borrowed from Your Grandchildren: The Evolution of 100-Year Family Enterprises* (Wiley, 2020), especially chapters 8–14.

34 Scharmer and Kaufer, *Presencing*.

35 Wesley, "The Blob."

36 Adam Grant, *Think Again: The Power of Knowing What You Don't Know* (Viking, 2021).

37 Jaffe, *Borrowed from Your Grandchildren*.

38 The learning we are advocating goes beyond education, cycles of incremental improvement, and skill-building toward something deeper: families and trust environments that support maturation, agency, and the lifelong process of becoming. The families' work is not primarily about learning more, but about growing up inside the structures that families create. In essence, they are creating a deliberately developmental organization (DDO), an idea developed by Robert Kegan and Lisa Laskow Lahey, renowned developmental psychologists at Harvard. To explore further, see Matthew Wesley, "The Developmental Family," Ascend, June 27, 2016, https://www.ascendfamilyadvisory.com/blog/801.

39 To explore further, see Hughes, Duke, Allred, "Reflection on Ghosts in a Family System," *FFI Practitioner*, May 26, 2026, on-line citation form: https://ffipractitioner.org/reflection-on-ghosts-in-a-family-system/.

40 For examples of families embracing "free choice," see Jaffe, *Borrowed from Your Grandchildren*, 272, 326.

Chapter 4 Resources for Further Learning

- Baumoel, Doug, Blair Trippe, and Katie Spencer. "The Progenitor's Dilemma: Avoiding Entitlement When Transferring Wealth: A Practical Framework That Empowers Heirs While Minimizing Negative Consequences." Continuity Family Business Consulting. Accessed January 23, 2026. https://continuityfbc.com/the-progenitors-dilemma-avoiding-entitlement-when-transferring-wealth.
- Brooks, Arthur C. *The Meaning of Your Life: Finding Purpose in an Age of Emptiness*. Portfolio, 2026.
- Burleigh, David W. *Take Ownership of What You Own: Build Your Confidence to Navigate the World of Trusts and Family Enterprise*. Windermere Press, 2024.
- Coyle, Daniel. *Flourish: The Art of Building Meaning, Joy, and Fulfillment*. Bantam, 2026.
- Edelman, Paul. "From Expert to Catalyst: Helping Families Build Decision-Making Confidence." Edelman & Associates. Accessed April 27, 2026. https://www.edelmancoaching.com/buildingdecisionmaking-confidence-articlebypauledelmanphd.

- Goldbart, Stephen, Stacy Allred, and Joan DiFuria. *The 10x10 Learning Roadmap: Advancing Flourishing in Families of Wealth*. James E. Hughes Jr. Foundation Publishing, 2024.
- Huizinga, Johan. *Homo Ludens: A Study of the Play-Element in Culture.* Martino Fine Books, 2024. This reprint of the 1955 edition is the classic evaluation of play, defined as the central activity in flourishing societies.
- Hughes, James E. Jr., and Keith Whitaker. "Building a Culture of Care in Trusts: Part I and Part II," *FFI Practitioner*, June 4, 2025, and June 11, 2025. https://digital.ffi.org/pdf/wednesday-edition/2025/june/june-04/building-a-culture-of-care-in-trusts-part-i.pdf and https://digital.ffi.org/editions/building-a-culture-of-care-in-trusts-part-ii/.
- Jaffe, Dennis. T., and James E. Grubman. *Cross Cultures: How Global Families Negotiate Change Across Generations*. FamilyWealth Consulting, 2016.
- Pink, Daniel H. *Drive: The Surprising Truth About What Motivates Us*. Riverhead Books, 2009.
- Stewart, Christian. "The Emerging Role of the Chief Learning Officer." Hidden Gem #9. The James E. Hughes Jr. Foundation. Accessed January 23, 2026. https://jehjf.org/hidden-gem-9-the-emerging-role-of-the-chief-learning-officer/.
- Taleb, Nassim Nicholas. *Antifragile: Things That Gain from Disorder*. Random House, 2012.

- Thomas, Buddy. *Love Wisdom Money: The Family Fiduciary's Guide to Generative Wealth*. Big Snowy Media, 2025.
- Wesley, Matthew, "Of Games and Culture", October 17, 2015, https://www.ascendfamilyadvisory.com/blog/701.

Chapter 5 Endnotes

41 Doug Baumoel and Blair Trippe, *Deconstructing Conflict: Understanding Family Business, Shared Wealth and Power* (Continuity, 2016).

42 Families need to be aware of and build strategies to navigate the trend of "higher intolerance of uncertainty." See, for example, Margaret Heffernan, *Uncharted: How to Navigate the Future* (Avid Reader Press, 2020). Heffernan argues that the future is inherently unpredictable, so the smarter move is not to perfect forecasts but to build preparedness: cultivate robust networks, run small experiments, practice scenario thinking, and institutionalize learning (premortems and after-action reviews). In a family system, Heffernan's approach translates to collective sense-making across generations, option-rich plans (small, reversible "safe-to-try" initiatives), and governance norms that reward updating beliefs as new evidence emerges. The goal is resilience and adaptability rather than false certainty.

43 For learning curriculum across 10 individual life stages (ages 5–100) and across 10 core competencies (group learning), see Stephen Goldbart, Stacy Allred, and Joan DiFuria, *The 10x10 Learning Roadmap: Advancing Flourishing in Families of Wealth* (James E. Hughes Jr. Foundation Publishing, 2024).

44 Emerging evidence suggests that gratitude promotes prosocial behavior, strengthens social bonds, and increases relationship satisfaction across close relationship, including family contexts. See Y. Joel Wong, "The Catalyst Model of Change: Gratitude Interventions with Positive Long-Term

Effects," *Affective Science* 4, no. 1 (2022): 152–162, https://pubmed.ncbi.nlm.nih.gov/37070004/.

A gift is incomplete without the expression of gratitude; thus, a powerful practice for beneficiaries (once or twice a year) is to write a gratitude letter to explain the types of positive impact the trust has had on your life and what you have learned from your experience as a beneficiary. The letter can be shared with a family member, a trustee, or if the trust creator is deceased simply written and placed in a file. The act of expressing gratitude contributes to becoming an active recipient. Hartley Goldstone, James E. Hughes Jr., and Keith Whitaker, "Beneficiaries and Trust Creators," in *Family Trusts: A Guide for Beneficiaries, Trustees, Trust Protectors, and Trust Creators* (Wiley, 2016), chap. 7, especially page 65.

45 Baumoel and Trippe, *Deconstructing Conflict*. This is an excellent resource for families to understand how conflict is inflamed and what can be done to moderate it in families. The authors refine the "spectrum of difference" to distinguish between disagreements, disputes, conflict, and cutoffs. See also Continuity Family Business Consulting at https://continuityfbc.com/.

46 The *personne de confiance* is a well-established concept in French law and healthcare, with a growing presence in family governance literature as a model for trusted advisors. See James E. Hughes Jr., "A Reflection on the Nature and Practice of the Role of the Personne de Confiance in a System of Family Governance; Historically and Today," (2005), The James E. Hughes Jr. Foundation, https://jehjf.org/a-reflection-on-the-nature-and-practice-of-the-role-of-the-personne-de-confiance-in-a-system-of-family-governance-historically-and-today/.

For an Eastern perspective, see Roger King, Winnie Qian Peng, and Christian Stewart, "The Family Office: The Glue to Keep Chinese Families Together," *FFI Practitioner*, August 24, 2016, https://ffipractitioner.org/the-family-office-the-glue-to-keep-chinese-families-together/.

47 "Jay Hughes on the Role of Elders in Flourishing Families," *Crafting Solutions to Conflict*, podcast, hosted by Jane Beddall, episode 258, December 6, 2023, https://craftingsolutionstoconflict.com/podcast/episode-258-jay-hughes-on-the-role-of-elders-in-flourishing-familiesnbsp. See also Jay's two reflections on elders at The James E. Hughes Jr. Foundation, accessed April 27, 2026: "A Reflection on the Role of Elders in a System of Family Governance," https://jehjf.org/a-reflection-on-the-role-of-elders-in-a-system-of-family-governance/; "A Reflection on the Traits and Capacities of Family Elders," https://jehjf.org/a-reflection-on-the-traits-and-capacities-of-family-elders/.

48 The four intangible capitals are based on Jay's original ideas first published in James E. Hughes Jr., *Family Wealth: Keeping It in the Family* (NetWrx, 1997). For the capitals in action, see Scott Peppet's "A 5 Capitals Self-Assessment Tool," Scott Peppet, accessed April 27, 2026, https://scottpeppet.com/articles/a-5-capitals-self-assessment-tool/.

Chapter 5 Resources for Further Learning

- Cheng, Jeremy, Kevin Au, Marta Widz, and Marshall Jen. *The Governance Marathon: Dynamic Durability in Entrepreneurial Families amid Disruptions*. 2086 Society and Family Firm Institute, 2021.
- DeCiantis, Devin, and Ivan Lansberg. *The Enduring Enterprise: How Family Businesses Thrive in Turbulent Conditions*. PublicAffairs, 2024.
- Doorley, Scott, and Carissa Carter. *Assembling Tomorrow: A Guide to Designing a Thriving Future*. Ten Speed Press, 2024.
- Dowell, Cale, Benjamin Pascut, and Matthew T. Lee.

Flourishing Performance Indicators: A New Framework for Wealth and Legacy. December 19, 2025. https://humanflourishing.web.baylor.edu/sites/g/files/ecbvkj2151/files/2025-12/KFPI%20December%2019_2025.pdf. See also Human Flourishing Program at Harvard.

- Friedman, Edwin H. *Generation to Generation: Family Process in Church and Synagogue*. Guilford Press, 2011. Friedman's work teaches family leaders that the most transformative intervention is not fixing family members or problems, but rather developing their own capacity for self-differentiation, emotional maturity, and non-anxious presence—enabling them to become the stabilizing force that helps their entire family system toward health and resilience.
- Hamilton, Sara S., and Margaret Vaughan Cox. *Build an Enterprise Family to Last: Proven Strategies to Thrive Across Generations.* James E. Hughes Jr. Foundation Publishing, 2024.
- Heifetz, Ronald, Alexander Grashow, and Marty Linsky. *The Practice of Adaptive Leadership: Tools and Tactics for Changing Your Organization and the World*. Harvard Business Press, 2009.
- Kegan, Robert, and Lisa Laskow Lahey. *An Everyone Culture: Becoming a Deliberately Developmental Organization*. Harvard Business Review Press, 2016.
- Kegan, Robert, and Lisa Laskow Lahey, *Immunity to Change: How to Overcome It and Unlock the Potential in Yourself and Your Organization*. Harvard Business Review Press, 2009.

- Likierman, Andrew. *Judgement at Work: Making Better Choices*. Profile Books, 2025.
- McCullough, Tom, and Keith Whitaker, eds. *Wealth of Wisdom: Top Practices for Wealthy Families and Their Advisors*. Wiley, 2022.
- Peppet, Scott, See https://scottpeppet.com for a wonderful mix of articles and podcasts on the practice of family flourishing including the family office as a platform for flourishing.
- Senge, Peter M. *The Fifth Discipline: The Art and Practice of the Learning Organization*. Currency Doubleday, 1990.
- Senge, Peter M., Art Kleiner, Charlotte Roberts, Richard B. Ross, and Bryan J. Smith. *The Fifth Discipline Fieldbook: Strategies and Tools for Building a Learning Organization*. Currency Doubleday, 1994.
- Sutherland, Kate. *We Can Do This! 10 Tools to Unleash Our Collective Genius*. Belgrave Press, 2014.
- Tordini, Claudia E., and Richard S. Franklin, eds. *Family Wealth, Inheritance and Well-Being. Appanage*, 2025.
- Weiner, Jamie. *The Quest for Legitimacy: How Children of Prominent Families Discover Their Unique Place in the World*. Wiley, 2022.
- York, David R. *The Gift of Lift: Harnessing the Power of Stewardship to Elevate the World*. Koehler Books, 2022.

About the Authors

L-r: Mary Duke, Jay Hughes, and Stacy Allred

The authors bring more than 100 years of combined service to families navigating the opportunities and responsibilities of wealth. Their collaboration on *Family Flourishing* grew from a shared commitment to restore a fuller understanding of wealth—one that reaches beyond financial capital to encompass well-being itself. Their trialogue has resulted in this book.

Beyond their professional credentials, they are blessed with their own flourishing families, full of beauty and complexity. For them, flourishing is not theoretical but lived—approached with humility, curiosity, and a deep respect for families.

James "Jay" E. Hughes Jr. has devoted his career to serving families seeking to discover and fulfill their purpose. Through his landmark work on the Five Capitals,

Jay helped reshape the global conversation about wealth, advancing a broader understanding of holistic well-being across generations. He continues to advise families and family office leaders worldwide and serves as a guiding voice in the evolving field of family wealth. jay@jehjf.org

Mary Duke has dedicated her career to helping families translate the promise of wealth into practices that strengthen trust, purpose, and flourishing across generations. Drawing on deep experience in trusts and fiduciary practice, family enterprise leadership, governance, and learning, she has helped advance a more humane approach to wealth stewardship—one that joins sound structures with the development of judgment, identity, responsibility, and relationship. Mary serves families and their owned enterprises, private trust companies and family offices around the world, bringing a global perspective, cultural sensitivity, and commitment to turning intention into lived experience. mkduke@thehighrd.com

Stacy Allred serves as Managing Director and Head of Family Engagement and Governance at J.P. Morgan Wealth Management (J.P. Morgan Securities LLC /member FINRA and SIPC). Over the course of her career, she has helped multigenerational families build the skills, structures, and confidence needed to steward wealth wisely. Stacy's work sits at the intersection of governance, learning, and leadership, grounded in the belief that enduring wealth depends as much on the quality of relationships as it does on the management of assets. Stacy.allred@jpmorgan.com

The views expressed solely belong to the author and do not necessarily reflect the views of JPMorganChase.

For additional reflections and
resources from the authors
see “Family Flourishing” in the library
of the James E. Hughes Jr. Foundation website.

jehjf.org/family-flourishing/

For more books from the publisher on
family governance and generational well-being
see “Publishing” on the
James E. Hughes Jr. Foundation website.

jehjf.org/publishing/

All proceeds from this book go to the
James E. Hughes Jr. Foundation